HR HOW-TO

Harassment Prevention

Everything you need to know to prevent and resolve workplace harassment ...

by Marjorie A. Johnson, J.D.

CCHKnowledgePoint®
Essential HR Solutions

Publisher: Catherine Wolfe
Editorial Director: Jeanne Statts
Portfolio Managing Editor: Mike Bacidore
Contributing Editors: Jan Gerstein, J.D.
                        Joy Waltemath, J.D.
Production Coordinator: Danford A. Miller
Cover Design: Craig Arritola, Laila Gaidulis
Interior Design: Laila Gaidulis
Layout: Publications Design

This publication is designed to provide accurate and authoritative information in regard to the subject matter covered. It is sold with the understanding that the publisher is not engaged in rendering legal, accounting, or other professional service. If legal advice or other expert assistance is required, the services of a competent professional person should be sought.

ISBN 0-8080-0949-4
©2003 **CCH** Incorporated
4025 W. Peterson Ave.
Chicago, IL 60646-6085
1 800 248 3248
hr.cch.com

Acknowledgements

There are numerous individuals who made the creation of this book possible. I'd like to thank CCH management and marketing for their support of this book and for choosing me to author it. I'd like to also recognize the many individuals whose research and expertise into this subject matter provided a strong foundation as this book was written. Special thanks to Joyce Gentry for her wisdom on discrimination prevention, and to the several outside experts whose names appear throughout this publication.

I would like to express my gratitude to Jan Gerstein and Joy Waltemath, whose editorial contributions to this publication are countless. Thanks also to Dan Miller for his careful attention to detail during the production process, to Laila Gaidulis for her unique design and creative cartoon illustrations, and to Craig Arritola for his artistic cover design.

Lastly, thank you Mark for your unconditional support and encouragement.

Marjorie Johnson
February 2003

Contents

Chapter 1   Introduction to harassment prevention 1

Chapter 2   Protected traits 13

Chapter 3   Understanding harassing conduct 27

Chapter 4   Sexual harassment..41

Chapter 5   Employer liability 65

Chapter 6   Policy creation and communication 79

Chapter 7   Anti-harassment training...97

Chapter 8   Managers and supervisors:
             special concerns and challenges...........................115

Chapter 9   Investigating harassment 127

Chapter 10   Resolution and corrective action 151

Chapter 11   Diversity initiatives 167

             Index..187

Introduction to harassment prevention

Why worry about harassment?..2

BEST PRACTICES: Audit your anti-harassment efforts.................2

What is a bias-free workplace?..3

Costs of harassment..4

    Hidden costs...4

    Litigation costs...5

    Damages...6

HR's role 9

The Quiz... 11

In the past week, two managers have come to you concerned about possible workplace harassment situations. One manager overheard a sexually charged conversation between a mixed group of workers. The other manager observed anti-Arab literature on a worker's desk. Nobody has complained to either manager about potential harassment. Of course, this could not have happened at a worse time. The organization is currently going through a reorganization and you're completely swamped with paperwork and meetings. Moreover, the HR office is understaffed and overworked due to a recent downsizing. What responsibility does HR have to take measures that will help prevent harassment from occurring? How is HR expected to respond if harassment is observed? If you choose to wait until your time frees up to do anything about the potential harassment, what's the worst that could happen? After all, nobody is complaining, right?

Why worry about harassment?

Harassment and other types of unlawful discrimination can have devastating effects in the workplace. Managers and supervisors who engage in workplace harassment subject their employers to automatic liability, regardless of whether HR condones the conduct or is even aware of it. Non-supervisory employees who engage in harassment can also subject their employer to liability if HR or management knows or should know about the conduct and fails to take prompt action to stop it. In addition to the potential financial costs of lawsuits brought by victims of harassment, an employer that allows harassment in the workplace often suffers the more "hidden" costs of lowered employee morale, negative publicity and high turnover.

HR's best defense is an offense. HR must see to it that action is taken to prevent and eliminate workplace harassment. This means creating, communicating and strictly enforcing a strong policy against harassment and other inappropriate conduct. It means responding promptly to complaints or observations of harassment and correcting a not-so-good situation before it gets very bad. When HR is made aware of workplace harassment or sees behavior that is inappropriate, it must swiftly address the complaint or stop the conduct. It must take all allegations seriously, and never dismiss a complaint as trivial.

A+ Best Practices

Audit your anti-harassment efforts

Ask yourself the following questions to determine whether your employer's anti-harassment efforts really protect the organization and its employees. You should be able to answer "yes" to each item.

- Do you have a policy in place that clearly defines acceptable workplace behavior?
- Is that policy communicated effectively throughout the workplace, using workplace communication from posting to face-to-face discussion?
- Do you train at least annually, including employees and management, and monitor the results of that training to confirm their understanding?

- ◆ Do you maintain records of that training?
- ◆ Are your complaint procedures designed to encourage people to come forward? Do they provide many avenues for reporting inappropriate behavior?
- ◆ Does management's actions reinforce what is stated in your policy?
- ◆ Is every complaint taken seriously, reported appropriately, and investigated aggressively?
- ◆ If harassment is found, do you take immediate action to remedy it?
- ◆ Do you follow up to make sure that harassment does not continue?
- ◆ Do you protect against retaliation?

What is a bias-free workplace?

Under federal law, employees have the right to work in an environment that is free from discrimination and harassment on the basis of a protected characteristic—race, religion, national origin, sex, age, veteran status and disability. Some states protect other characteristics, such as sexual preference or marital status. Harassment on the basis of a protected characteristic is illegal when the conduct at issue is so severe so as to create a "hostile environment."

This does not mean that employers are required to act fairly toward employees in some general or abstract sense. What it does mean is that employers must maintain a bias-free workplace—a working environment that is free of discrimination and harassment based on these specific characteristics. This includes taking reasonable measures to control or eliminate the overt expression of those prejudices in the employment setting.

HR can and should enforce policies that set higher standards by prohibiting all types of conduct that may be offensive to a member of a protected class. Any time offensive conduct is allowed in the workplace, the employer risks morale problems and turnover as well as the potential disruption and expense of a harassment lawsuit.

WHAT you need to know

Costs of harassment

There are many ways in which an employer will "pay" for allowing a work environment that tolerates or condones illegal discrimination and harassment. There are the hidden costs—such as lowered morale and harm to the organization's reputation—as well as the well-known and very publicized legal costs.

Hidden costs

Lawsuits aren't the only reasons why HR should be doing all that it can to stop workplace harassment and discrimination. In today's highly competitive global market, there are the hidden costs of workplace harassment. In many ways, these hidden costs may prove to be much more expensive than a lawsuit.

Lost productivity and lowered morale. Workplace harassment can cost an employer lost productive time. Allegations of harassment in the workplace can be very disruptive. For one, harassment limits the ability of the victim to contribute to the organization. Moreover, other employees who observe or learn about the harassment become upset. If HR does nothing to address the problem, it can be demoralizing to employees. Absenteeism and turnover will likely follow.

Harm to reputation. When harassment claims are made public, the employer's reputation in the community will suffer. Business opportunities may be lost, and good job applicants may avoid seeking employment with the organization. Current employees may seek other opportunities.

DON'T miss this

The internal reputation of the organization also suffers. An employer that allows harassment to occur is, in effect, undermining its vision, its mission and its core values. After all, an employer can hardly boast that "our people are our most important asset," yet allow workplace harassment and other inappropriate behavior to occur.

Litigation costs

Probably nobody would argue that defending a harassment lawsuit can be quite expensive. Because of the high costs associated with going to trial, it is simply bad business sense for HR *not* to take proactive measures to prevent and eliminate workplace harassment. Two of the highest costs associated with litigation are the cost of settlement and the cost of taking a case to trial.

Settlements. In order to prevent harm to business and personal reputations, employers often settle claims of workplace harassment quickly. Oftentimes parties hire a mediator to help negotiate a settlement. The mediator's fees, in addition to the organization's attorneys' fees, can really add up. In short, settlements can be quite costly compared to the cost of taking proactive steps to prevent potential harassment.

WHAT you need to know

Every HR practitioner has no doubt heard about the multi-million dollar settlements reached by the EEOC in class action lawsuits alleging a pattern and practice of racial or sexual harassment. But these high-profile cases are actually quite uncommon. What is more concerning are the less publicized—but much more frequent—costly settlements involving less insidious harassment, such as the EEOC's settlement of:

◆ Male-on-male harassment suit against an auto chain for $500K.
◆ Sex and race harassment suit against a chicken processing plant for $485K.
◆ Race harassment suit against a Florida citrus grower for $249K.
◆ Racial harassment suit against a global manufacturer and distributor of paper and building products for $200K.
◆ Race harassment suit against a Louisiana car dealership for $200K.
◆ Sexual harassment suit against a retailer for $115K.

Costs of going to trial. Regardless of whether an employer wins or loses a harassment lawsuit, it will potentially spend hundreds of thousands of dollars defending the case. Indeed, the high cost of litigation is often the reason that cases settle early, even if an employer believes it has a strong defense. Two of the most expensive litigation costs are fees paid to the attorneys and to the expert witnesses.

◆ **Attorneys' fees.** An employer's attorneys' fees often represent the highest cost of litigation and are born by the organization regardless of whether it wins or loses the case. It is rare for the employee to have to pay these fees, even if he or she loses the case.

◆ **Expert witness fees.** Employers often hire expert witnesses to help assist them in defending a harassment lawsuit. For example, an expert may be hired to testify about the employee's realistic loss of future earnings or his or her psychological well being.

WHAT you need to know

Even if an employer has legal coverage through employment practices liability insurance, most insurance carriers will require that the covered employer have in place a preventive anti-harassment program.

Damages

Above and beyond the costs of going to trial are the monetary damages that an organization will be forced to pay if the victim who is suing wins.

Types of damages. An employer that loses a discrimination or harassment suit may be ordered to pay the victim:

◆ Back wages for any lost time at work as a result of the harassment.

◆ Reimbursement for any past monetary losses (for example, doctor's bills or money spent seeking another job).

◆ Compensatory damages for emotional harm suffered as a result of the harassment (including mental anguish, loss of enjoyment of life and inconvenience); as well as future monetary losses (such as those expected due to inability to work or future medical expenses).

◆ Punitive damages to punish the organization for wrongdoing.

◆ Future wages (if reinstatement is not feasible under the circumstances).

◆ The victim's attorney and expert fees.

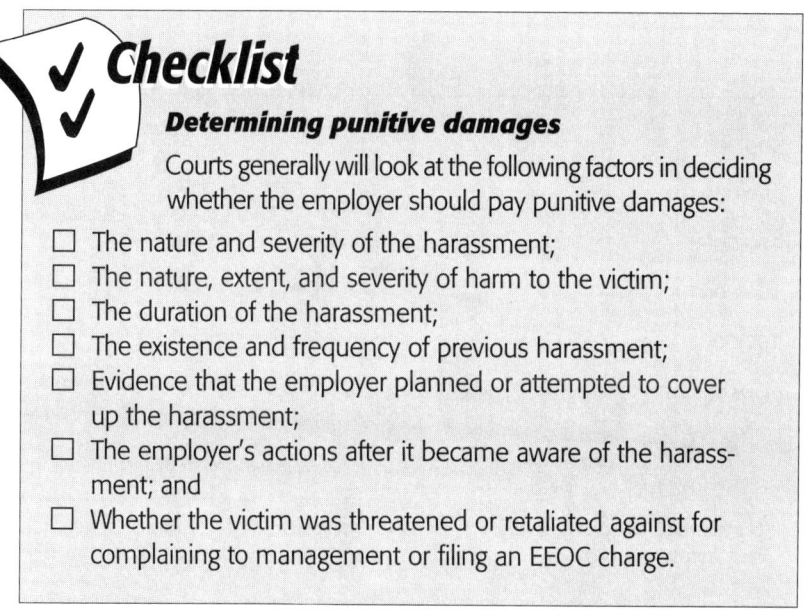

✓ *Checklist*

Determining punitive damages

Courts generally will look at the following factors in deciding whether the employer should pay punitive damages:

☐ The nature and severity of the harassment;

☐ The nature, extent, and severity of harm to the victim;

☐ The duration of the harassment;

☐ The existence and frequency of previous harassment;

☐ Evidence that the employer planned or attempted to cover up the harassment;

☐ The employer's actions after it became aware of the harassment; and

☐ Whether the victim was threatened or retaliated against for complaining to management or filing an EEOC charge.

What kind of money are we talking? Like most legal questions, "it depends." There have been cases in which employers have been ordered to pay monetary damages in the millions of dollars. However, it seems more often that damages will range in the hundreds of thousands.

According to one report, the median jury award in discrimination cases over a seven-year span was $150,000. However, the average jury award has shown a startling progression over the years. The average award in 1994 was $93,000, which increased to $150,000 in 1997 and was $218,000 in 2000. Of all discrimination types, age discrimination plaintiffs won the most money from 1994-2000, with a median compensatory award of $268,926. The median for disability cases was $175,001, compared to cases involving racial discrimination at $120,951 and sex-discrimination cases at $100,000.

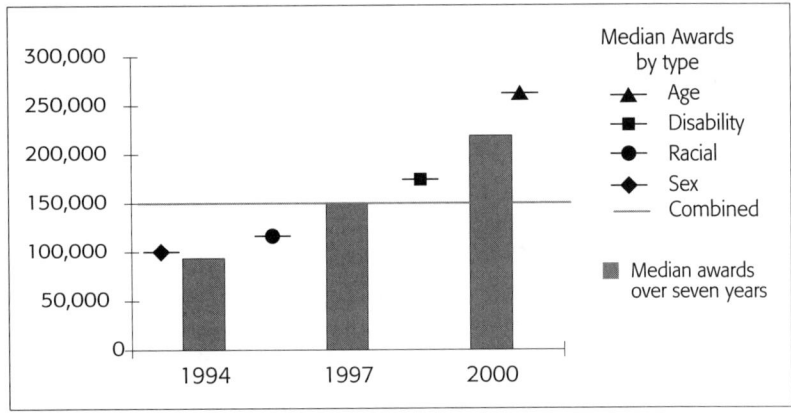

(Jury Verdict Research's annual Employment Practice Liability: Jury Award Trends and Statistics report).

Think back to the two managers who have told you about potentially harassing situations. As you can see, doing nothing may prove quite costly. It is imperative that HR find the resources to investigate the two matters to determine whether harassment is occurring so that appropriate action can be taken to restore a harassment-free environment. This may mean appealing to upper-level management for additional resources. Or, it may mean putting other tasks on the back burner so that you can focus on promptly investigating and resolving the reported incidents. If HR chooses to ignore the potential harassment, you may very well regret it.

HR's role

How HR prevents and reacts to workplace harassment will play an important role in helping an employer avoid both the legal and hidden costs of harassment. The following is a set of guidelines to follow in order to help reduce and possibly avoid the chance of harassment occurring in your organization. As you proceed through the chapters of this book, you will gain more detailed information pertaining to each of these guidelines.

1. Issue a strong policy against harassment. Write the policy so that all employees can understand it. Define and provide examples of hostile environment harassment, including sexual harassment, and make the explanation of prohibited conduct very clear. Explain the disciplinary sanctions up to and including discharge that will be applied to harassers.

2. Outline a complaint procedure. Make it easy for employees to report harassment or other inappropriate workplace behavior. Provide several avenues so that the employee has the ability to bypass his or her supervisor, who might be the alleged harasser.

3. Communicate the policy. Distribute and regularly and clearly communicate the policy to employees and document that you have done so. Redistribute the policy periodically. Post the policy in central locations and incorporate it into employee handbooks.

4. Train employees. Educate all employees, including supervisory staff, to recognize and confront harassment. Emphasize their responsibility to report harassment should it happen to them, and explain how they should do so. Keep records of attendance at training sessions.

5. Train managers and supervisors. Supervisory staff should receive additional training on how to enforce the policy and to be sensitive to improper conduct. Instruct all supervisors and managers to address or report all complaints of harassment, even if the complaint does not conform to the complaint procedures.

6. Monitor managers and supervisors. Include EEO preventive practices as part of a manager's or supervisor's job responsibilities. Keep track of supervisory personnel's conduct to make sure that these folks are carrying out their responsibilities.

7. Investigate every complaint. Do not assume that a complaint is not important. All harassment claims must be taken seriously and investigated promptly and thoroughly by an impartial investigator. Investigators should be well trained in the skills that are required for interviewing witnesses and evaluating credibility.

8. Maintain confidentiality. Maintaining confidentiality assists in encouraging employees to come forward with complaints and also reduces the risk of a defamation lawsuit.

9. Act immediately to stop harassment. Correct apparent harassment, regardless of whether a complaint has been filed. Adopt a remedy that will be effective to end the harassment. Restore any job benefits or opportunities to the victim that were lost because of the harassment and offer appropriate counseling or other compensation for losses. Discipline the harasser in a manner that reflects the severity of the conduct.

10. Follow up periodically. It is important that the remedy has been effective to stop the harassment and that no retaliation has been taken against the victim or witnesses.

11. Document the investigation. Develop and keep accurate records of all details of a harassment investigation. Preserve the complete record in a safe, confidential manner for a period of time that is at least as long as any regulatory or state statute of limitations that may apply.

12. Stop retaliation immediately. Failure to stop reprisals against an employee who complains of harassment or someone who participates in a harassment investigation can result in liability for an employer, regardless of the outcome of the investigation. The employer should follow up periodically to ensure the retaliation does not occur again.

The Quiz

1. Which of the following is *not* a hidden cost of workplace harassment?
   a. Decreased turnover.
   b. Lowered morale.
   c. Lost productivity.
   d. Harm to employer's reputation.

2. If an employee sues her employer for racial harassment and wins, the employer may be ordered to compensate her for which of the following:
   a. Lost wages.
   b. Emotional suffering.
   c. Attorneys' fees.
   d. All of the above.

3. If HR is aware of workplace conduct that is offensive, but probably not unlawful harassment, it should do nothing to stop it.   ❑ True   ❑ False

4. Settlement of a harassment lawsuit is often an inexpensive alternative to trial.   ❑ True   ❑ False

Answer key: 1.a, 2.d, 3.F, 4.F.

Protected traits

Federal law protects certain traits 14

Race, color and national origin 15

    Slurs and threats 16

    English-only rules.. 17

    Non-minorities... 19

    BEST PRACTICES: Preventing harassment

      in a time of international conflict 19

Gender.. 20

Religion 21

Disability 21

Age 23

Veteran status 23

Pregnancy and childbirth 24

State law protections 24

The Quiz... 25

Pedro, a front-line supervisor, asks you for some help. He keeps getting complaints from several employees about one of his team leaders, Raffi. Just yesterday two workers on Raffi's team, Dwayne and Beverly, complained to Pedro about Raffi's leadership. And this isn't the first time. Last month two other team members, Glenn and Kao, also complained. The general consensus seems to be that Raffi is rude and doesn't offer needed assistance to any of the team members. Pedro wants to know whether he should treat the situation as a simple performance management issue or if he needs to be concerned about possible harassment. What does HR need to consider before advising Pedro?

Federal law protects certain traits

Workplace harassment and other forms of discrimination must be on the basis of a "protected characteristic" to be illegal. Why? Because several federal laws prohibit employers from discriminating against individuals on the basis of certain "protected characteristics." In other words, the laws restrict the criteria an employer may use when making employment decisions. The protected characteristics, and the primary federal laws, are as follows:

- ◆ Race, color, national origin, gender and religion (Title VII of the Civil Rights Act of 1964).
- ◆ Disability (Americans with Disabilities Act).
- ◆ Age (Age Discrimination in Employment Act).
- ◆ Veteran status (Uniformed Services Act).
- ◆ Pregnancy and childbirth (Pregnancy Discrimination Act).

WHAT you need to know

Abusive conduct that targets gays or lesbians solely because of their sexual preference (as opposed to their gender) is not unlawful under federal law, even if the conduct clearly creates a hostile work environment. But note that it may be unlawful under state or city law. For more information about sexual-orientation harassment, see Chapter 4.

Contrary to what many workers would like to believe, federal law does not in fact require that an employer treat all employees fairly or politely. It only protects from discrimination and harassment those workers who are members of the protected classes identified above.

> ***Example 1:*** *Suppose an African American employee working on an offshore drilling rig is subjected to crude jokes and pranks by coworkers. If all of the workers are equally subjected to such crude jokes and pranks, and there is no racial hostility in the interplay, the employee has not been the subject of racial harassment.*

> **Example 2:** *Consider a supervisor who subjects a female employee to abusive language. If the supervisor subjects all employees, male and female, to the same abusive behavior, the supervisor has not engaged in illegal gender harassment. Nevertheless, the supervisor's conduct may violate the employer's bias-free workplace policy requiring respectful behavior. It also demonstrates poor leadership qualities.*

Think back to Pedro and Raffi. It certainly appears that Raffi needs to be counseled about his leadership style. But it doesn't initially seem that there is a harassment problem. HR needs to work with Pedro to be sure that Raffi isn't singling anyone out because of his or her membership in a protected class. If Raffi does target everyone with his crass behavior, regardless of any protected traits, this is a performance and/or discipline issue.

Race, color and national origin

Race and ethnicity are among the most frequent objects of workplace harassment. Inappropriate conduct can range from:

- ◆ **open hostility** (for example, name-calling and racial slurs);
- ◆ **sending a negative message** that persons of a particular race or ethnicity are inferior and unwelcome (for example, the placement of Ku Klux Klan literature in an employee's work area); to
- ◆ **subtle put-downs** (for example, a team of financial planners who address non-minority members as "Mr." or "Ms." in the presence of clients, but who refer to minority members by their first name).

In a study conducted by the Fair Employment Council of Greater Washington, it was determined that at least one in five Hispanic job applicants encounters some type of discrimination based on their ethnicity. The study concluded that not only do Hispanics encounter discrimination, but male Hispanics are twice as likely to experience discrimination as female Hispanics. The study also revealed that discrimination was more likely to occur for positions that required less than a college degree.

DON'T miss this

Slurs and threats

Racial or ethnic slurs, jokes or demeaning statements that are sufficiently severe so as to be perceived as hostile or abusive will create a racially hostile work environment. Usually isolated incidents, even if clearly motivated by discriminatory intent, are not sufficiently severe to be unlawful. However behavior that is exceptionally abusive or threatening, such as one case where workers twice hung a noose over an employee's work area, may rise to the level of unlawfulness.

Worst case scenario

Increasing racial harassment complaints

Since the late 1990s, the EEOC has seen a disturbing national trend of increased racial harassment cases involving hangman's nooses in the workplace, noted EEOC Chairperson Ida L. Castro during remarks to the 91st Annual Convention of the National Association for the Advancement of Colored People (NAACP) in July, 2000.

Castro also noted that charges of racial harassment filed with the EEOC had increased from 1.5 percent of all charges (9,757) in the 1980s, to 6 percent of all charges (47,175) in the 1990s. EEOC lawsuits alleging racial harassment increased more than ten-fold from two such lawsuits in 1996 to twenty-two in 1999.

Solution. HR should clearly communicate to all employees—either through a written policy or other appropriate mechanism—that harassment such as ethnic slurs or other verbal or physical conduct directed toward any racial, ethnic, or religious group is prohibited and that employees must respect the rights of their coworkers. Effective and clearly communicated policies and procedures should be in place for addressing harassment complaints. Managers should be trained on how to identify and respond effectively to harassment even in the absence of a complaint.

English-only rules

Your manufacturing company employs many workers who speak Vietnamese. HR is ready to implement work teams. A team leader, Caleb, asks to have a rule that only English may be spoken during team meetings and on the production floor during working time. HR has concerns as it suspects that there may be a negative reaction from the employees. Also, can't English-only rules can be a sign of discrimination? Should HR approve Caleb's request?

Rules requiring that employees speak only English at all times in the workplace may disadvantage employees on the basis of national origin and can create an atmosphere of inferiority, isolation and intimidation that results in a discriminatory or harassing working environment.

The EEOC takes the position that English-only rules applied at all times are presumptively discriminatory, although the courts have not always agreed with that approach. When a rule is applied at certain times (for example, only on the production line), it must be justified by a business purpose in order to avoid discrimination or harassment claims. Rules applied during work time only are less likely to be considered harassment and more likely to show a business purpose.

What should HR do about Caleb's request?

◆ **Decide whether an English-only rule is necessary.** HR should first consider whether there really is a language problem. As long as the employees who speak Vietnamese are not interfering with the organization's efficiency or causing tensions with other employees, there might not be any harm for certain employees to converse in another language. It may, in fact, be easier for employees to speak in their primary language and it may boost their morale to be able to do so, especially during the transition period to teams.

◆ **Determine if an English-only rule is a business necessity.** It has been shown that the use of another language at work may adversely affect efficiency, job performance, safety, teamwork, customer service, management-employee communications and racial/ethnic tension. In such cases, an English-only rule has been found to be a business necessity.

HR may find that Caleb believes that requiring employees to speak English at all team meetings and while working would ensure that all employees and supervisors could understand each other during meetings and that it would prevent injuries through effective communication on the production floor. He may also believe that it would prevent non-Vietnamese employees from feeling that they were being talked about by Vietnamese employees. Such reasons suggest that there is a business purpose for an English-only rule.

◆ **Is everybody fluent in English?** The use of English may be difficult for some employees. If HR is uncertain whether a Vietnamese employee understands instructions or information provided in English, it should make sure that the instructions or information is also explained in Vietnamese. Also, HR could arrange for the company to offer English classes to employees whose primary language is not English.

◆ **Communicate the rule to employees.** Should HR decide to implement an English-only rule, employees need to be told about it—who it applies to, when it applies, what languages are involved, and what the consequences are for violating the rule. It should be explained in all employee communications, discussed in training programs and management guides, and it should be posted. HR should notify employees of the rule in both English and the language with which the employees are most comfortable. HR should also consider a grace period before the rule becomes effective in order to ensure that employees have received actual notice of the rule.

◆ **Enforce the rule fairly.** It is best that HR counsel employees when there are rule violations as opposed to automatically disciplining a violation. The rule must be enforced in a manner that does not create a hostile environment.

DON'T miss this

*Remember that hostility toward persons in a protected class may be unintentional. Conduct that has the **effect** of creating a hostile or offensive work environment can be illegal, regardless of intent.*

Non-minorities

Can non-minority employees experience racial or ethnic harassment? Yes. Workers who are offended by the harassment of others have an equal right to work in an environment that is free from harassing or discriminatory conduct. Non-minority workers may become a target for discrimination through association, such as an employee who is harassed because of an interracial marriage. Caucasian workers can be subjected to racial harassment, particularly in a predominantly non-White workplace.

A+ *Best Practices*

Preventing harassment in a time of international conflict

The EEOC has expressed concern for individuals who are members of, or are perceived to be members of, religions, countries or ethnic groups that are at risk of reprisal following the September 11, 2001 terrorist attacks.

Anger at those responsible for the terrorist attacks should not be misdirected against innocent individuals, urges the EEOC. Be particularly sensitive to potential harassment against individuals who are (or who are perceived to be) Muslim, Arab, Afghani, Middle Eastern or South Asian. The EEOC specifically warns against four certain types of harassment:

1. **Affiliation.** Harassing an individual because he or she is affiliated with a particular religious or ethnic group. For example, harassing an individual because she is Arab.

2. **Physical or cultural traits and clothing.** Harassing a worker because of physical, cultural or linguistic characteristics, such as accent or dress associated with a particular religion, ethnicity or country of origin. For example, harassing a woman wearing a hijab (a body covering and/or headscarf worn by some Muslims).

3. **Perception.** Harassing an employee because of the belief (correct or not) that he or she is a member of a particular racial, national origin or religious group. For example, harassing a Sikh man wearing a turban because the harasser thought he was Muslim.

4. Association. Harassing an individual because of his or her association with a person or organization of a particular religion or ethnicity. For example, harassing an employee whose husband is from Afghanistan.

Gender

Inappropriate conduct that is based on a person's gender may be sex discrimination. Sexual harassment is one type of gender-based discrimination. Because sexual harassment presents special concerns and considerations, it is covered in greater detail in Chapter 4.

But sexual harassment is not the only type of conduct based on sex that may be unlawful. Non-sexual behavior that shows hostility towards a particular gender may be unlawful harassment. For example, profane or vulgar language of a nonsexual nature may be harassment if it is used in the presence of or directed toward members of one sex only.

✓ ✓ Checklist

Examples of gender harassment

According to the EEOC, nonsexual conduct that may be the basis of unlawful gender-based discrimination when based on the gender of the person subjected to it includes:

- ☐ Offensive language, including vulgar or profane language.
- ☐ Physical conduct, such as obstructing one's path or pushing.
- ☐ Berating an individual for mistakes.
- ☐ Criticizing work performance.
- ☐ Strict enforcement of absence or tardiness rules.
- ☐ Removing duties or responsibilities.
- ☐ Additional work.
- ☐ Forbidding conversation with coworkers.
- ☐ Refusal to instruct.
- ☐ Failure to cooperate.

Example: *Barbara and Fran worked in an office in which their manager threatened them, restricted their work assignments, denied them overtime, and placed other standards of conduct upon them that were different than their male coworkers. A court held that this conduct, although not sexual in nature, could constitute an unlawful hostile work environment.*

Religion

Harassment because of religion may not be as common as gender, racial or ethnic harassment, but it is equally inappropriate. Religious harassment may occur if an employer allows someone to "preach" a particular religion to workers or to condemn another's religion. Although a coworker's simple invitation to church services may not be inappropriate in itself, repeated unwelcome invitations could create a hostile environment.

Worst case scenario

The preaching supervisor

A supervisor might create a hostile environment if employees are forced to attend staff meetings opened by prayer or religious talks, or if performance reviews are linked with religious conversations.

Solution. HR needs to ensure that supervisors and managers are particularly careful about advocating religious ideas. This is because such conduct could be especially intimidating given their position in the organization.

Disability

Hostile or demeaning conduct based on disability may rise to the level of unlawfulness and is certainly inappropriate for the workplace.

Worst case scenario

Worker with mental disability suffers harassment

An employee with schizophrenia is constantly referred to as a "lunatic" and a "nut case," and coworkers go out of their way to put the individual in stressful interpersonal situations that aggravate the mental condition. This conduct, if severe and persistent, could constitute unlawful harassment.

Solution. To help avoid disability discrimination and harassment, managers and workers should be sensitized to the concerns of people with disabilities.

A new awareness about disabilities will not come about automatically, although exposure to individuals with disabilities should do a lot to change attitudes. Two steps HR should take are to:

◆ conduct training of managers, supervisors and employees to develop more realistic attitudes; and

◆ teach the appropriate disability language and the skills to interact with people with disabilities (disability etiquette).

Who is an individual with a disability? An individual with a disability is a person who has a physical or mental impairment that "substantially limits one or more of the person's major life activities; has a record of such impairment; or is regarded as having such an impairment." The EEOC has also taken the position that excessive questioning or imposition of medical examinations may constitute disability-based harassment prohibited under federal law.

WHAT you need to know

Under federal law, the term "disability" does *not* include:

◆ homosexuality or bisexuality;

◆ compulsive gambling, kleptomania, or pyromania;

◆ psychoactive substance use disorders resulting from current use of illegal drugs; or

◆ transvestism, transsexualism, gender identity disorders not resulting from physical impairments or other sexual behavior disorders.

Age

Older workers may be objects of harassing or inappropriate conduct. Federal law protects individuals who are 40 years of age or older from discriminatory conduct based on their age.

While courts have held that isolated remarks by supervisors might not rise to the level of unlawful harassment, any employer who permits or encourages—even in jest—teasing related to a person's age, may face a lawsuit.

> **Example 1:** *Betty is a 50-year-old bank teller whose younger coworkers openly and frequently tell jokes about her age and medical problems, although they never discuss their own health or medical problems. Betty has asked them to stop, but they tell her that she's just too sensitive—another trait that they attribute to her age. The coworkers may be engaging in illegal harassment; at the very least their conduct is inappropriate for the workplace.*

> **Example 2:** *Mark is 48 years old and works on a loading dock. Mark's coworkers are always making jokes about the "old man" and leave the largest and heaviest boxes for him. They also changed the computer settings for the shipment tracking system so that information was displayed in extremely small print. Like Betty in the example above, Mark may be a victim of age harassment.*

Veteran status

Federal law prohibits employees from being discriminated against because of past, current or future military obligations. Although the courts have not considered the issue often, this would seemingly include workplace harassment.

Individuals who are protected from discrimination include those who:

WHAT you need to know

- ◆ served in the past in a uniformed service and were honorably discharged;
- ◆ currently are a member of, or are serving in, a uniformed service;
- ◆ have an obligation to perform such service; or
- ◆ are an applicant for membership in a uniformed service.

Pregnancy and childbirth

Federal law prohibits discrimination in the workplace on the basis of pregnancy and childbirth. The law mainly protects female applicants or employees from being treated differently than a male applicant or employee because of the female's pregnancy or capacity to become pregnant.

In terms of employment decisions, leave policies and benefits, an employer is required to treat pregnancy and related medical conditions the same as other disability conditions are treated. Workplace harassment on the basis of pregnancy could also violate federal law.

State law protections

States and local municipalities may protect additional characteristics not protected by federal law. The more common of these protected characteristics include:

◆ Homosexuality/sexual preference;

◆ HIV/AIDS;

◆ Marital status;

◆ Parenthood; and

◆ Use or non-use of lawful products, such as alcohol, tobacco and/or prescription drugs.

❓The Quiz

1. Hostile or demeaning conduct based on a person's
   _____ may be unlawful under federal law.
   a. Age.
   b. Race.
   c. Hair color.
   d. All of the above.
   e. Choices a and b.

2. In some states, employees are entitled to   ❏ True   ❏ False
   be free from discrimination and harassment
   because of their sexual preference.

3. Which is an example of possible unlawful harassment?
   a. Colleagues referring to all coworkers by their first names
      instead of as "Mr." or "Ms."
   b. Younger coworkers intentionally leaving the heaviest boxes
      for an older coworker to carry.
   c. A supervisor who refers to all of his subordinates as "idiots."

4. A woman who is constantly ridiculed by   ❏ True   ❏ False
   her coworkers because she is married
   to a man with schizophrenia may be
   a victim of disability-based harassment.

Understanding harassing conduct

When is behavior harassment?... 28

    Discrimination vs. harassment 28

    Hostile environment 28

Look at all the circumstances 29

    Factors to consider... 29

    Isolated incidents... 31

Types of conduct 31

    Verbal and written abuse... 31

    Physical conduct and threatening behavior 32

Inappropriate computer use 33

    The Internet 33

    E-mail 34

    BEST PRACTICES: E-mail management plan
        helps derail online harassment 35

Managers and supervisors 36

Non-employee harassment... 37

Off-work conduct 38

The Quiz.. 39

One of your line managers, Mina, calls you with some disturbing information concerning one of her direct reports, Doreen. Six months ago Doreen informed HR that she suffers from Parkinson's Disease. HR has been working closely with Doreen and her doctor to provide her with a reasonable accommodation that will enable her to continue working at the facility. Mina has noticed that in the past several weeks, Doreen has become isolated from the group. Mina used to see Doreen occasionally chatting with coworkers in the hallway and eating lunch with others in the cafeteria. Now she rarely sees Doreen talking to other workers and often observes her eating lunch alone at her desk. Last week Mina noticed two workers walk right by Doreen without saying a word. What really concerns Mina is that yesterday she overheard a coworker comment that "it's not fair that Doreen is getting special treatment," and that she should "just go home and collect disability." Could Doreen be a victim of harassment?

When is behavior harassment?

A group of federal laws makes it unlawful for most employers to discriminate against any individual with respect to terms and conditions of employment because of that person's race, religion, gender, national origin, age, disability or veteran status. These protected characteristics are discussed in more detail in Chapter 2.

Discrimination vs. harassment

Discriminatory conduct is any form of verbal or physical conduct that undermines the employment relationship, that interferes with an employee's ability to perform his or her job, or that creates an intimidating, hostile, or offensive work environment. *It includes harassment*, which consists of any conduct that degrades or shows hostility to another because of his or her race, religion, gender, national origin, age, disability, veteran status, or any other category protected by law.

Hostile environment

Illegal harassment because of a protected characteristic occurs when the harassment is enough to create a "hostile environment." A hostile environment exists when:

◆ An employee has been subjected to verbal or physical conduct that shows hostility toward an employee because of a protected characteristic; and

◆ The conduct has the purpose or effect of interfering with the employee's work performance or opportunities, or creating an intimidating, hostile or offensive work environment.

Set higher standards. HR can set higher standards for employees that exceed the limits of workplace behavior allowed by the law. For example, a claim of hostile environment workplace harassment usually requires several instances of abusive behavior. But HR can make it policy that not even one instance of abusive behavior will be allowed and that anyone engaging in inappropriate behavior in the workplace will be subject to discipline, even if the behavior does not meet the legal definition of unlawful workplace harassment.

Not all conduct that is offensive or even vulgar violates the law. But tolerating offensive conduct because HR thinks it is not severe enough to constitute unlawful harassment is never a good idea. What is offensive but legal one day may not be legal the next day. Any time offensive conduct is allowed in the workplace, an employer risks the disruption and expense of a harassment lawsuit.

Look at all the circumstances

To the dismay of many HR practitioners, there is no mathematically precise test for determining whether conduct based on a protected characteristic has created a hostile environment. Courts view the conduct from both a subjective and objective viewpoint. The subjective test examines whether the victim actually perceived the conduct to be severe or pervasive enough to create a hostile or abusive environment. The objective test looks to whether the victim's subjective perception is a reasonable one.

Factors to consider

The best approach to use in evaluating whether specific behavior has created a hostile environment—the one followed by the courts and the EEOC—is to examine all the circumstances. Key factors HR should consider include:

◆ The nature of the conduct (physical, verbal, or both);
◆ The identity of the perpetrator(s) (supervisor, coworker, or even nonemployee);
◆ Whether the conduct was physically threatening or humiliating, or merely an offensive comment;

- The frequency, severity and pervasiveness of the conduct;
- The context(s) in which the conduct occurred;
- Whether the conduct was unwelcome (uninvited by and offensive to the victim); and
- Whether the conduct unreasonably interfered with an employee's work performance.

This is not a complete list of factors to consider. There may be other pertinent circumstances to take into account in a particular case. And, remember that although the conduct in question may not constitute what is legally defined as workplace harassment, an employer may set higher standards of workplace behavior than just what is "illegal."

WHAT you need to know

There is no requirement that a person be fired, demoted, lose promotion opportunities or suffer some other sort of economic or monetary harm in order to sue an employer for unlawful workplace harassment. Employees are entitled to work in an environment that is free from intimidation, ridicule or insults based on their membership in a protected class.

Think back to Doreen, who has become isolated from her group ever since she made known her disabling condition. In gathering facts to determine whether Doreen may be a victim of disability-based harassment, HR should consider the severity of the coworkers' conduct and whether it is unreasonably interfering with Doreen's ability to do her job. Also, are only coworkers engaging in the behavior or are supervisory employees involved? Is the behavior unwelcome?

Find out who seems to be initiating Doreen's isolation. Has she chosen to keep to herself or have her coworkers chosen to keep their distance? Finally, keep in mind that even if the coworkers' behavior does not rise to the level of unlawfulness, it may be inappropriate. HR should take steps to help ensure that Doreen is able to work in an environment free from hurtful behavior. The fact that a coworker is unhappy that Doreen is receiving an accommodation should alert HR that bias-free training might be in order.

Isolated incidents

A single incident or isolated incidents of offensive behavior generally will not create a hostile environment, unless the conduct is quite severe. One remark that results in offended feelings usually will not be unlawful. But the remarks should still be stopped when brought to the attention of HR. Deal with isolated or minor instances of inappropriate conduct in accordance with their severity.

> Isolated or infrequent incidents of extremely offensive conduct, particularly when perpetrated by a supervisor or when coupled with physical conduct, might be sufficient to create a hostile environment.

WHAT you need to know

Types of conduct

Verbal and written abuse

Perhaps the most common type of harassment is verbal abuse. In its most direct form, verbal abuse consists of epithets, slurs or jokes directed against individuals because of protected characteristics.

But verbal harassment may be subtler. Comments that were never intended to show bias can still create a hostile work environment. For example, referring to male employees as "men" and female employees as "girls" may be gender harassment because the implication of female inferiority inherent in the different treatment can lead to a hostile or offensive work environment. Similarly, there may be racial or ethnic harassment when non-minority males are referred to as "men" while minority males are called "boy."

DON'T miss this

> *Even berating a coworker for mistakes or criticizing his or her work performance can be discriminatory if it is based on membership in a protected class. It can also amount to harassment if it interferes with an employee's work performance or creates an intimidating, hostile or offensive work environment. An example would be a supervisor's statements berating an older employee's performance, such as, "I should have know you'd do a bad job with this. After all, you can't teach an old dog new tricks."*

Demeaning impersonations. Verbally or physically impersonating another employee can create a hostile environment, especially if this is done in conjunction with other potentially objectionable conduct. Examples include a worker who:

◆ mimics a Russian immigrant's accent while criticizing his work performance;

◆ pretends to use a cane while walking behind an older coworker; or

◆ duplicates the distinctive speech pattern of a person with a cognitive disability while talking about the person in front of coworkers.

Offensive writings. Written derogatory remarks are just as inappropriate as spoken remarks. Demeaning or insulting drawings, cartoons, slogans and symbols can also create an offensive environment and are inappropriate.

Physical conduct and threatening behavior

Inappropriate physical conduct may include obstructing a person's path, pushing, shoving, grabbing or touching. Destruction of a person's equipment or work product can also be harassment when done because a person belongs to a protected class.

Physical conduct is frequently associated with intimidation, which is always inappropriate. Physical conduct of a sexual nature is addressed in greater detail in Chapter 4.

Intimidation. Acts of intimidation have a threatening quality. The threats may be explicit or implicit. Threatening conduct is serious. When based on a protected characteristic, it may constitute unlawful harassment. Such behavior is highly inappropriate and HR should never tolerate it.

WHAT you need to know

Specific acts of intimidation do not have to be frequent to create a hostile environment. A single instance of particularly severe or offensive conduct can be harassment. For example, an African American employee who finds a noose hung over his work area could be the target of racial harassment on the basis of that one act. Disciplinary action would be commensurate with the severity of the conduct.

Refusal to cooperate. Another form of inappropriate conduct is a refusal to assist or cooperate in work that requires a team effort. The conduct is discriminatory and may be harassment when directed at a person because of a protected characteristic.

Inappropriate computer use

In order to provide a safe, nondiscriminatory work environment, HR should prohibit use of e-mail or the Internet to send, receive or access obscene, pornographic or discriminatory material.

What does this mean? Prohibit the sending of any messages that contain material that is, or possibly could be, interpreted as abusive, sexist, racist or otherwise offensive. This especially includes any messages that could be considered sexual harassment, such as sexually suggestive material that is hostile to a particular gender. Another example is repeated and unwanted requests for a date. Make it known that your policies on equal opportunity and sexual harassment do apply to e-mail messages and Internet activities.

Smoking gun e-mail has become so common in workplace lawsuits that 9.4 percent of US companies have been ordered by courts to produce employee e-mail, according to a survey from the American Management Association, The ePolicy Institute and US News & World Report. Morover, 8.3 percent have battled sexual harassment and/or sexual discrimination claims stemming from employee e-mail and/or Internet Use (2001 Electronic Policies and Practices Survey).

The Internet

The Internet allows users immediate access of information from all around the world. Obviously, this can be a very valuable resource. However, it also has the potential for negative consequences in the workplace. Because the World Wide Web is not regulated, it contains information that some users may find offensive. Thus, there are areas on the Internet that are simply inappropriate for access by employees. Misuse of the Internet can affect productivity or decrease morale.

Certain misuse can subject the employer to legal liability. Therefore, never allow Internet use to access sites with themes that are sexual, racist or otherwise discriminatory. Prohibit workers from downloading pornographic or violent material, such as sexually suggestive graphics or screen savers.

DON'T miss this

The AMA's 2001 Electronic Policies and Practices Survey revealed that, among companies that allow personal Internet use, 65.3 percent restrict access to Web sites, with 76.6 percent most concerned about keeping explicit sexual content off employees' screens.

E-mail

Just as with other types of communications, sending offensive jokes or material over an employer's e-mail system might contribute to the creation of a hostile work environment. Some examples include:

- ◆ derogatory remarks about a person's race, sex, age, religion, national origin or disability;
- ◆ offensive, degrading sexual comments or jokes; and
- ◆ pornographic or obscene material.

Special concerns about managers. A manager or supervisor who sends or receives harassing or discriminatory messages via e-mail places their employer at great risk for legal liability. Sexist, racist or otherwise offensive material found to have been sent or received by managers or supervisors could very well help the plaintiff to win his or her case.

Indeed, such online behavior by managers or supervisors can result in automatic liability. Even if it does not, the uncovering of offensive material will prove embarrassing and expensive to the organization. A manager may not have intended a joke forwarded to a friend via e-mail to be viewed as harassing or discriminatory, but his or her intentions probably will not matter to a judge or jury. The same holds true for Internet sites visited. The expert may be able to retrieve a history of sites accessed by managers and supervisors through the employer's computer.

Best Practices

E-mail management plan helps derail online harassment

If your employees have computers and those computers are connected to the Internet, you have a potential legal battlefield at every workstation, warned Janet Goldberg McEnery of Macfarlane, Ferguson & McMullen in Tampa. Speaking at the 2000 SHRM Conference in Las Vegas, McEnery urged HR professionals to have an e-mail management plan. The problem, she explained, is not e-mail in general, but unmanaged e-mail.

As part of your e-mail management plan, make sure that employees do not have an expectation that their business e-mail is a method of private communication, said McEnery. HR has the responsibility to make the rules on how, when and for what it is used. She recommends the following steps.

◆ Have an express written policy for e-mail use and enforce it.

◆ Make sure everyone understands that just because an e-mail message has been deleted does not mean it is gone forever.

◆ Allow reasonable personal use of your e-mail if you wish.

◆ Have employees acknowledge in writing that they understand your e-mail use policy.

◆ Train your employees and supervisors on appropriate e-mail use.

◆ Make it clear that you will periodically review employee e-mail files.

◆ Stress that passwords are not confidential, but that employees should not share their passwords with others.

◆ Interface your e-mail and harassment policies.

◆ Coordinate e-mail and record-keeping retention practices.

◆ Take corrective action when e-mail is abused.

Managers and supervisors

The severity of inappropriate conduct is increased when committed by a manager or supervisor. Because managers and supervisors have authority over employment decisions, their harassing conduct is more likely to intimidate employees and interfere with their work performance. Employees are less likely to complain or ask a manager to stop harassing conduct.

Moreover, statements made by supervisors can be directly attributed to the employer. Supervisors are considered to be agents of the employer. Any statements made by a supervisor can be attributed to the employer and used as evidence to show that an employer acted improperly in firing an employee. Thus, supervisors should be careful to make statements that are only related to their job of managing people to meet the organization's goals.

WHAT you need to know

> If a supervisory employee engages in harassment, the employer may be automatically or "vicariously" liable for the harassment. This means that the employer will be liable even if HR never even knew about the harassment. For more information on employer liability, see Chapter 5.

Harmful behavior

Discriminatory or harassing behavior by supervisors and managers may take additional forms, including:

- ◆ **Assignment.** Intentionally assigning persons in a protected class to menial or exceptionally strenuous job tasks—making them do "grunt" work—is discriminatory and has been recognized as a mode of unlawful harassment.
- ◆ **Surveillance.** Discrimination and harassment may also take the form of special surveillance of a worker on the basis of a protected characteristic. Supervisors must not use race, religion, gender, national origin, age, disability or veteran status as a reason to pay closer attention to a person's absences, tardiness or personal time on the telephone, for example.

- **Training.** A refusal to train, or substandard or inadequate training, directed at persons because of membership in a protected class is also discriminatory and can amount to harassment. A person who is discharged for poor work performance may be entitled to reinstatement if the reason for his or her poor performance was discrimination in training.
- **Discipline.** Excessive and inconsistently harsh discipline because of an employee's protected trait is discriminatory conduct and may be harassment.
- **Forced quit.** Subjecting an employee to conditions that are so intolerable that a reasonable person would feel compelled to resign is a form of harassment. That the employee has voluntarily quit is not a defense to discrimination charges.

Non-employee harassment

Unlawful harassment may be committed by third parties in the workplace, such as customers, sales representatives, subcontractors, repair workers or independent contractors.

In determining whether an employer should be responsible for harassment by a third party, courts will look at whether:

1. the employer knew or should have known of the conduct;
2. the employer had some control over the situation or was otherwise legally responsible for the non-employee's conduct; and
3. the employer failed to take immediate and appropriate corrective action.

Worst case scenario

Maribeth works as a waitress. When she asked if the four male customers seated at her table were ready to order, one man put his arm tightly around her waist and told her what he wanted was not on the menu, prompting his companions to laugh and comment in the same vein. When Maribeth was finally able to finish taking their orders, the man removed his arm and patted her as she turned to leave. She went directly to the restaurant manager and reported the unwelcome sexual conduct.

Solution. The employer may be responsible if, on learning of the sexual harassment, it fails to take immediate and appropriate corrective action within its control. Depending on the circumstances, such action might be relatively simple—for example, switching table assignments. In this case, the manager should arrange to have a waiter finish serving that table and making whatever arrangement might be necessary so that Maribeth would not be financially or otherwise harmed by the substitution (for instance, by losing the amount of a tip she could have earned).

Off-work conduct

While employment-related harassment usually occurs in the everyday workplace, it can also occur outside of the normal work environment. Typical situations include:

- ◆ Employer-sponsored social events—for example, at an employer-sponsored holiday party or sporting event.
- ◆ Private locations not related to work—for example, after-work drinks at a local bar, restaurant, or hotel.
- ◆ Customer locations—for example, during a sales call at a customer's office.
- ◆ Cyberspace—for example, while checking email or accessing a work-related online bulletin board.

The Quiz

1. To bring a lawsuit for workplace harassment,   ❏ True   ❏ False
   a victim does not need to show that he or
   she suffered any monetary or economic harm,
   such as being fired or demoted.

2. Factors that HR should consider in determining whether specific
   behavior has created a hostile environment include:
   a. The severity of the conduct.
   b. The frequency of the conduct.
   c. Whether the conduct unreasonably interfered with an
      employee's work performance.
   d. All of the above.

3. An isolated incident will never create a   ❏ True   ❏ False
   hostile work environment.

4. Which of the following is a true statement that HR should
   consider when it prohibits the sending of offensive material over
   an employer's e-mail system?
   a. Personal use of e-mail should always be banned
      in the workplace.
   b. The sending of offensive e-mail could contribute to the
      creation of a hostile work environment.
   c. Even if an employee or supervisor deletes offensive e-mail,
      the message may be still be later retrieved.
   d. Both choices b and c.

Answer key: 1.T, 2.d, 3.F, 4.d.

Sexual harassment

Introduction	**42**
Legal background	**43**
Unwelcome sexual conduct	**43**
Guard against "tolerated" behavior	**44**
Hostile environment sexual harassment	**45**
What is hostile?	**45**
Are compliments wrong?	**47**
Isolated incidents	**48**
Participation in the conduct	**48**
Supervisor sexual harassment	**50**
Same-sex and sexual orientation harassment	**51**
Dating in the workplace	**52**
Dangerous liaisons	**53**
Take workplace romances seriously	**54**
BEST PRACTICES: Managing office romances	**56**
State law considerations	**57**
State legislation	**57**
The Quiz	**63**

Seth, one of the managers at your organization, stops by your office. He tells you that he just finished speaking to Jennifer, an employee who approached him with a complaint of sexual harassment. Jennifer told Seth that two of her male coworkers, Roger and Juan, often make off-color, sexual jokes in her presence. She also told him that they make comments about the appearance of other women in the office. Jennifer said that she is very uncomfortable by the conduct and doesn't know what to do. Seth informs you that he has spoken briefly to Roger and Juan about the situation. The two admitted that they sometimes joke around but said that they had no idea

Jennifer was upset. In fact, according to the two men, Jennifer often comments on her own sex life in response to their questions. Could Jennifer be a victim of sexual harassment? Does it matter whether Jennifer did in fact join in the sexual banter? How can you determine whether the conduct is unwelcome? What should you do next?

Introduction

By now, every HR professional is very aware that employers must take action to prevent and eliminate sexual harassment in the workplace. Nobody wants the EEOC knocking at the door with a charge of sexual harassment.

However, keeping the workplace free of inappropriate sexual behavior can be a challenge in the modern workforce. Despite preventative measures throughout corporate America, sexual harassment continues to plague the workplace. Charge statistics released by the EEOC report that the agency received 15,475 charges alleging sexual harassment in 2001. Additionally, a 1999 survey released by the Society for Human Resource Management (SHRM) found that internal complaints of sexual harassment are on the rise, despite the widespread existence of written policies, prevention training and establishment of investigative procedures. Responses were received from 469 HR professionals.

DON'T miss this

According the SHRM survey, of the 1,214 sexual harassment complaints that the HR respondents stated were filed between 1995 and 1998:

- ◆ 15 percent were received in 1995;
- ◆ 23 percent were received in 1996;
- ◆ 32 percent were received in 1997; and
- ◆ 30 percent were received within the first nine months of 1998.

Legal background

Why is sexual harassment illegal? Because it is a form of gender discrimination, which is specifically prohibited by federal and state law.

The earliest court cases that found sexual harassment to be unlawful involved male supervisors who requested sexual favors from female workers. Often, the woman would be fired or be forced to quit if she refused the supervisor's sexual advances. The woman became a target of her male supervisor's sexual advances *because* she was a woman. The supervisor would not place similar sexual demands upon male subordinates. This was gender discrimination, courts held.

Courts soon expanded the definition of sexual harassment to include more than sexual demands by supervisors. Jokes, pinups, graffiti, vulgar or abusive language, innuendoes, negative gender stereotyping, sexist slurs, references to sexual activity, or overt sexual conduct by fellow workers were held to be unlawful sex discrimination. As explained in Chapter 2, federal law gives employees the right to work in an environment free from intimidation, insult or ridicule based on race, sex, religion or national origin. Sexual harassment that creates a hostile work environment for members of one sex is every bit the arbitrary barrier to sexual equality in the workplace that racial harassment is to racial equality.

Unwelcome sexual conduct

Sexual harassment in the workplace occurs when any employee is made to feel uncomfortable because of sexual conduct at work that is unwelcome.

Sexual harassment is often subtle. Therefore, it's not always easy to decide whether sexual harassment has occurred. Believe it or not, behavior can be offensive, it can be rude, it can be demeaning, but it may not be sexual harassment. Also, sensitivities of people differ. What one person may think is funny, someone else may think is inappropriate and unwelcome.

Like other forms of workplace harassment, sexual harassment is viewed by the perception of the victim. In other words, sexual or gender-based conduct in the workplace is unwelcome when an employee does not solicit or initiate the conduct and when the employee reasonably regards the conduct as undesirable and offensive. It does not matter whether the person engaging in the conduct would consider the behavior offensive. All that matters is whether the individual on the receiving end reasonably finds it offensive.

Guard against "tolerated" behavior

Problems can also occur where an individual's acceptance of sexual behavior appears to be voluntary, but that person is in fact very offended by the conduct, warned Jackson Lewis attorney Michael Lotito at the HumanAssets.org 2000 Show & Conference. A person may "tolerate" sexual behavior yet not "welcome" it.

For example, a person may tolerate unwelcome behavior out of fear that he or she will be retaliated against for complaining. Therefore, it is important that an employer's policy makes clear that retaliation is prohibited.

Other reasons why an individual may choose not report unwelcome behavior include:

- ◆ Fear of coworkers ("Nobody will talk to me anymore if I complain").
- ◆ Self-blame ("I must have said or done something to indicate I welcomed this behavior").
- ◆ Reluctance to get a coworker in trouble ("I think he's a creep, but don't want him fired because then his family will suffer").
- ◆ Concern about violent behavior ("I'm afraid of what he'll do if he finds out I went to management").

Because these are such powerful motivations to tolerate unwelcome sexual behavior, HR must ensure that its managers and supervisors are proactive about acting to eliminate sexual behavior whenever they see it occurring, advised Lotito. If harassment is in public view and an employer's supervisors knew or should have known about it, the organization will be legally responsible.

Hostile environment sexual harassment

Hostile environment sexual harassment occurs when unwelcome sexual conduct in the workplace is "severe and pervasive" and "unreasonably interferes with an employee's ability to do his or her job," or "creates an abusive environment." That's the legal standard, but what do these terms mean in the context of your workplace?

An isolated incident will rarely be considered to create a hostile environment. Similarly, conduct that is rude or insulting, although inappropriate for the workplace, will not rise to the level of sexual harassment. Because there is often a fine line drawn by the courts between what is "severe and pervasive" and what is not, it is best to put in place a policy that requires everyone in the workforce to refrain from conduct that reasonably could be considered offensive to others.

> **Example:** *Ritu is a member of a software sales team consisting of herself and four men. The group often goes out for drinks after work on Thursday nights, along with a male vice-president of a major client. Because Ritu works on the vice-president's particular account, she feels compelled to attend the "happy hour." After business talk is over, the conversation often turns sexual, with the men joking about their sexual conquests and commenting about the appearance of other women in the restaurant. Often, they ask Ritu about her sex life and ridicule her when she blushes. A couple of times, the group has left to go to a local tavern where the servers are scantily dressed women. Each time, Ritu has declined the men's invitation to "tag along." This pattern of behavior is inappropriate, and if unwelcome, could be considered by Ritu to be a sexually hostile work environment.*

What is hostile?

Some examples of hostile environment sexual harassment include:
- ◆ Obscene or "dirty" remarks or jokes.
- ◆ Sexual gestures—winking, whistling, kissing sounds.
- ◆ Pornographic materials—paperweights, nude or semi-nude photographs, calendars featuring semi-nude persons in sexual poses, obscene cartoons.

◆ Inappropriate touching—rubbing shoulders, hugging, grabbing.

◆ Sexual advances—repeatedly asking someone out on a date, kissing, grabbing.

◆ Comments of a sexual nature about a person's weight, body shape, clothing, and the way they walk, talk or sit.

◆ Acts of physical aggression or intimidation—yelling, shouting, pushing.

◆ Talking about the sexual activities or desires of the harasser, harassee or other person, including comments or questions about the sensuality of the person or his or her spouse or significant other.

WHAT you need to know

There is no requirement that a person be fired, demoted, lose promotion opportunities or suffer some other sort of economic or monetary harm in order to sue his or her employer for sexual harassment. Employees are entitled to work in an environment that is free from intimidation, ridicule or insults based upon their gender. Unwelcome sexual conduct that unreasonably interferes with the ability of a person to work or that creates an intimidating, hostile or offensive working environment can constitute sexual harassment, regardless of whether a monetary loss occurred.

Ask yourself... HR can respond to all inappropriate conduct that may lead to a claim of sexual harassment by asking the following questions concerning the behavior. If the answer to any of these questions is "no," take action to stop the behavior.

◆ Would you want the same thing said or done in front of your spouse, sibling, child or parent?

◆ Would you normally say or do the same thing to a member of your own sex? (for male/female harassment)

◆ Did it need to be said or done at all?

◆ Did it serve any useful business purpose?

◆ Would you want to be seen on the national news saying or doing it?

Think back to Jennifer. Once you have investigated Jennifer's allegations, ask yourself whether Roger and Juan's behavior was appropriate. If sexual comments were indeed being made, it's quite doubtful they belong in the workplace, and appropriate measures should be taken to stop the behavior and prevent it from occurring in the future. This is true even if you determine that the conduct does not rise to the level of illegal sexual harassment.

Remember, too, that employers can be sued for more than just "sexual harassment" if the sexually harassing conduct qualifies as wrongful under state "common law" and some state employment discrimination laws. Multimillion-dollar awards have been issued in these types of cases, because more damages—both compensatory and punitive—are available than for just sexual harassment claims.

✓ *Checklist*
✓

Types of wrongful conduct

Types of misconduct that can arise in sexual harassment charges include:

- ☐ Assault and battery—touching without permission.
- ☐ Intentional infliction of emotional distress—knowing and continued pressure after indication action was "unwelcome."
- ☐ Loss of consortium—loss of ability to have consensual sex.
- ☐ False imprisonment—forced to remain in an area and unable to avoid unwelcome advances.
- ☐ Invasion of privacy—questions asked were an unreasonable intrusion into personal life.
- ☐ Wrongful discharge—failure to stop harassment forced the victim to quit.

Are compliments wrong?

Sexual harassment does not include occasional compliments of a socially acceptable nature. Sexual harassment is conduct that is not welcome or that is personally offensive and fails to respect the rights of others. An occasional compliment usually does not meet this definition.

Perceived harassment is often the result of a misunderstanding between the parties. Employees may not know that their conduct is objectionable. Actions that may appear harmless or amusing to one person may be offensive to another. Also, behavior that may be appropriate or overlooked away from work may constitute sexual harassment on the job.

For example, most people would agree that telling an employee on occasion that she looks nice is not offensive. However, the result might be different if that employee is a subordinate and instead of telling him that he looks nice, his supervisor tells him he looks really "hot." A male manager who frequently places his hand on the shoulder of a female subordinate while discussing a work project with her may be comfortable with this action. The female subordinate, however, may find it embarrassing, intimidating or simply uncomfortable.

Isolated incidents

Sexual harassment, whether physical, verbal, or both, usually requires a pattern of ongoing offensive behavior. Isolated incidents of offensive behavior, although inappropriate, generally are not sexual harassment.

It's different when it's the boss, however. When it is a manager or supervisor who commits sexual or gender-based conduct, the severity increases. Just one unwelcome touching of an employee's intimate body area by a supervisor may create a hostile environment. Similarly, single incidents of extremely offensive sexual verbal conduct by a supervisor could also be deemed sexual harassment.

Participation in the conduct

In some circumstances, a person who has engaged in sexual talk at work can still be a victim of sexual harassment. Remember, when determining whether sexual harassment has occurred, the question is whether or not the conduct is welcome.

Past use of vulgar language or sexual innuendo cannot be used to show that an employee would never be offended by sexual comments or that such conduct is generally welcome. An employee may willingly participate in sexual or gender-based conduct, but then stop. Sexual harassment can be found if the employee tells coworkers or other people involved that the conduct is no longer welcome.

Worst Case Scenario

A tinsmith shop's only female, Mary, was subject to daily harassment by the men in the shop who were unhappy about working with a woman. The men referred to Mary in derogatory terms and subjected her to offensive signs, pictures and graffiti. Mary was also the target of various gender-related pranks, and twice a coworker deliberately exposed himself. Mary complained to her supervisor about the conduct for almost four years before she finally quit and sued the company for sexual harassment.

At trial, the company argued that the harassment was not unwelcome because Mary herself used vulgar language and engaged in "unladylike" behavior. The court rejected this argument since Mary had made it clear through her complaints that the conduct was unwelcome and in light of the fact that she was just one woman against many men. Because there was no evidence that Mary enjoyed or appeared to enjoy the harassment, her participation in the sexual nature of the work environment did not defeat her claim.

Solution. Sexual joking or innuendo—welcome or unwelcome—is inappropriate in the workplace. An employer is inviting trouble if it tolerates such behavior. Comments by one person should not be regarded as an invitation for the rest of the workforce to join in. All comments of a sexual nature observed by HR, managers or supervisors should be stopped immediately. Employees should be told that such conversations are not appropriate for the workplace.

Remember Jennifer? She told her manager Seth that she did not welcome the sexual environment created by Roger and Juan. But it's possible that she engaged in sexual banter herself. How must HR respond?

- ◆ **Investigate.** First and foremost, investigate the situation promptly and take any necessary action to remedy potential harassment (see Chapter 9 about investigations and Chapter

10 about remedying workplace harassment). Keep in mind that even if Jennifer did join in some of the sexual talk, her behavior does not necessarily mean that she welcomed the sexually charged environment. By complaining to Seth, Jennifer has clearly indicated the conduct is not welcome.

◆ **Train.** Based on Jennifer's complaint, now would be a good time to reeducate the workforce about harassment (see Chapter 7). To avoid being perceived as welcoming sexual conduct, employees who no longer want to participate in workplace "sex talk" should be encouraged to firmly tell others that they no longer want to participate.

◆ **Report.** If the conduct continues or an employee feels uncomfortable confronting his or her coworkers, the employee should be strongly urged to report the behavior to management by following the complaint procedure set forth in the employer's sexual harassment policy. And it should be well understood that if an employee tells a coworker or group of employees that they wish sexual banter to stop—the employees must immediately stop.

Supervisor sexual harassment

Sexual harassment by supervisors is particularly damaging. As explained in Chapter 5, if a manager or supervisor engages in workplace harassment that violates federal law, the employer faces automatic liability. And, if a manager or supervisor fails to stop sexual harassment that exists, the employer also faces legal trouble.

Remember that the severity of sexual conduct is increased when committed by a manager or supervisor. Because a supervisory employee has authority over employment decisions, his or her harassing conduct is more likely to intimidate employees and interfere with their work performance. Think about it; an employee is far less likely to complain or ask the harasser to stop if that person is a manager or supervisor.

"Quid pro quo" sexual harassment and tangible job actions.
One category of sexual harassment that was first recognized by the courts can be engaged in only by supervisory staff—*quid pro quo* sexual harassment. In the simplest sense, *quid pro quo* means "something for something." This happens when a harasser makes unwelcome sexual conduct a part of the job or the basis for an

employment decision—like firing an employee because he or she refuses to provide sexual favors.

Courts now have begun to shift their focus away from a *quid pro quo* analysis when supervisor harassment is involved. Instead, the EEOC and courts find it more useful to distinguish between harassment that results in a *tangible employment action* and harassment that creates a *hostile work environment* because the difference between the two determines whether an employer can defend itself against automatic liability.

> **Example:** *Amy reports directly to Cedric, who has the authority to discharge her. One day Cedric tells Amy that he finds her attractive and would like her to join him for dinner. Amy says "no thanks." A few days later, Cedric again asks Amy to join him for a dinner date. Amy turns down Cedric's second offer and tells him not to ask her again because she is not interested in him romantically and she is uncomfortable with his repeated requests for a date. Angered by Amy's rejection, Cedric terminates Amy the next day. Because Cedric terminated Amy for rejecting his sexual advances, he has engaged in unlawful quid pro quo sexual harassment.*

Same-sex and sexual orientation harassment

Same-sex harassment is against the law. Sexual harassment does not always involve a man harassing a woman. It is also unlawful for a man to sexually harass another man and a woman to sexually harass another woman. The only issue is whether the harasser is treating the victim a particular way because of his or her gender.

> *According to statistics released by the Equal Employment Opportunity Commission, the number of sexual harassment complaints filed by men has increased in recent years. In 2001, approximately 14 percent of sexual harassment claims were brought by men as opposed to women.*

DON'T
miss
this

Sexual orientation harassment can be illegal. Abusive conduct that targets gays or lesbians solely because of their homosexuality (as opposed to their gender) is not unlawful under federal law, even if the conduct clearly creates a hostile work environment. Although federal law prohibits discrimination on the basis of gender, it does not prohibit sexual orientation discrimination.

However, a number of states and municipalities have laws that do prohibit sexual orientation discrimination in the workplace. Also, depending on its severity, sexual orientation harassment can cause extreme emotional distress, which may also provide the basis for a lawsuit.

Even if an organization is not subject to a state or local law banning sexual orientation harassment, the employer can and should still set higher standards by prohibiting it in the workplace. Sexual orientation harassment can be just as hurtful to the victims and the workplace as sexual harassment.

DON'T miss this

Many gay and lesbian employees continue to experience persistent discrimination in the workplace, according to a national study conducted by Witeck-Combs Communications, Inc. and Harris Interactive. Two out of five gay and lesbian respondents to the on-line survey reported facing some form of hostility or harassment on the job, while one in ten stated that they were either dismissed from or pressured to quit a job because of their sexual orientation. In addition, 12 percent of those same respondents believed that they had been denied a promotion or job advancement based on sexual orientation.

Dating in the workplace

Louisa, a line worker at one of your off-site manufacturing plants, calls you on the phone early one morning. She tells you that she desperately needs some advice concerning a personal situation at work. Louisa proceeds to explain that she legally separated from her husband six months ago and subsequently has become romantically involved with her male supervisor, Chen. Louisa assures you that her and Chen have kept their relationship a secret and that there has been no negative effect on their working relationship. The problem, Louisa goes on to explain, is that she has decided to try to make things work with her husband and therefore plans to end her romance with Chen. Louisa is very concerned about how Chen will take the news and how the break up will affect her job since Chen is her boss. Currently, your company has no policy that specifically addresses dating in the workplace. How should you handle this situation?

A romantic relationship at the workplace is not, by itself, against the law. However, such an affair can be dangerous—especially if the relationship is between a manager or supervisor and a direct or indirect subordinate. The conduct between the parties can at any time cross the blurry line between legality and unlawful sexual harassment. Moreover, even though a relationship between a manager and a subordinate might not meet the legal definition of sexual harassment, employees may still be offended or disadvantaged by the relationship and may even take legal action.

Dangerous liaisons

Specific problems concerning manager-subordinate romances can develop when:

- ◆ The relationship is not welcome;
- ◆ Intimate actions occur at work;
- ◆ The relationship ends for one person but not for the other; or
- ◆ Preferential treatment is given to the subordinate.

The relationship is not welcome. Even if an employee consents to the sexual advances of a supervisor, the sexual conduct can still be unwelcome. An employee voluntarily may participate in unwelcome sexual conduct because the employee fears losing his or her job if the sexual advances are rejected. The law looks at whether the employee acted in a way that would indicate the sexual advances were unwelcome.

Intimate actions occur at work. A manager and subordinate who openly show affection at work run the risk of offending others and even making it more difficult for them to get their jobs done. And, even if an isolated kiss in the hallway or a sexually suggestive conversation between a supervisor and subordinate does not create a sexually hostile environment, it is inappropriate workplace behavior.

The relationship ends. Harassment can follow the break up of a supervisor-subordinate romance. A spurned supervisor's conduct toward an employee can quickly become unlawful harassment. What was previously welcome sexual behavior may no longer be welcome. And, if the supervisor takes a negative employment action against the employee as a result of the break up, the employer will be automatically liable if the victim sues. The fact that there was a prior consensual relationship between the parties will not prevent liability for sexual harassment when post-affair advances by a supervisor are unwelcome.

Preferential treatment is given to the subordinate. Favoritism or preferential treatment based upon the granting of sexual favors can create a hostile work environment for "innocent bystanders"—both male and female employees who are offended by the conduct. It does not matter whether the sexual conduct is directed at them or if the favorably treated employees are willing participants. When widespread favoritism sends a silent message to employees of one gender that the only way for them to get ahead is to participate in sexual conduct, the employer can be liable for sexual harassment.

Take workplace romances seriously

A strong sexual harassment policy that defines and provides examples of supervisor and hostile environment sexual harassment, and that makes clear that all managerial personnel are subject to it, can help to prevent manager-subordinate affairs from crossing the line to illegality. Employers can set even higher standards by prohibiting all sexual activity in the workplace and by prohibiting any sexual favoritism.

A prohibition on manager-subordinate relationships is another possibility, but such a ban may be impossible to enforce and may even infringe on employee privacy rights. Managers and supervisors must be knowledgeable of the employer's policy concerning manager-subordinate relationships.

A survey of HR and corporate executives conducted by the Society for Human Resource Management (SHRM) and CareerJournal.com found that very few organizations have formal policies on workplace romances. Of the 558 HR pros and 663 execs polled, 81 percent and 76 percent, respectively, deemed workplace romances dangerous because they can lead to conflict in the organization. Respectively, 76 percent and 71 percent said they would personally avoid workplace romances.

In contrast, 75 percent of HR pros and 59 percent of execs said their organizations had no policy on workplace romance. For those organizations that do, 64 percent of HR pros and 52 percent of execs said their organizations permitted, but discouraged, romance in the workplace. Different opinions emerged in potential challenges and consequences that may arise from a workplace romance. For example, 58 percent of executives said that workplace romances should be banned because of the potential for retaliation if the romance ends, while only 12 percent of HR pros gave that reason.

HR can also take precautions with respect to any known manager-subordinate relationship. For instance, both parties can be clearly warned of the potential dangers of the relationship and the boundaries on their conduct. Also, if favoritism, indiscreet conduct, or coercion is suspected, HR should investigate. In some cases, it may be feasible to transfer one of the parties in order to end their supervisory relationship. But any transfer should be done with the transferred party's consent and care should be taken that the same opportunities exist for the party in the new position.

To protect an organization from potential liability, a manager or supervisor that is involved in a romantic relationship with a subordinate should discreetly make this fact known to human resources or any other employer representative responsible for EEO-compliance practices. Appropriate action should then be taken to protect all those involved.

⚜ *Best Practices*

Managing office romances

Some attorneys advise employers that rigorous adherence to the organization's anti-harassment policy is the best protection, along with paying close attention to what happens when the relationship ends and making certain that the employee knows how to make complaints under the company's policy. Others recommend a policy that specifically addresses relationships between management and employees; it may require the couple to report the relationship to the company.

Attorney Brandon R. Blevans of the law firm of Littler Mendelson of San Francisco, California, advises employers to use consensual relationship agreements for protection. While they will not totally determine whether harassment occurred during or after the relationship, he says, they re-inform employees of their rights and obligations and provide HR with documentation, signed by both the manager/supervisor and the employee, that they will not engage in harassing behavior. HR should ask employees to *voluntarily* sign the agreements.

When the need for a consensual relationship agreement arises, other legal issues may be involved. Therefore, Blevans strongly recommends that HR consult with legal counsel before using a consensual agreement to ensure that it is appropriate for the circumstances.

Think back to Louisa and Chen, where Louisa had indicated that she intends to end her relationship with Chen, her supervisor. It would be prudent to speak with Chen promptly and let him know that HR is aware of the situation and is determining the best way to proceed. In order to ensure that any actions Chen may take as a supervisor concerning Louisa are not perceived as retaliatory, it may be best to end the managerial relationship as quickly as possible. If Louisa is transferred from Chen's group, make sure that you have her consent and that she does not view the transfer as retaliation.

Follow up regularly with both Louisa and Chen to make sure that no future issues arise. Now may be the time to consider a policy about workplace dating, at the very least requiring or encouraging managers and supervisors to make known any intimate relationships with subordinates.

State law considerations

Employers have two potential areas of concern with state laws addressing sexual harassment. First, state laws may specifically require employers to do specific acts (and these laws vary from state to state). Second, employers may be subject to lawsuits filed in local courts that aren't strictly sexual harassment claims, like assault and battery, intentional infliction of bodily harm, and other related allegations. These kinds of claims may involve individuals as well as the organization, and may have criminal as well as civil penalties. Consequently, it's critical for HR to know what the law is in each state where the organization has employees.

State legislation

State laws vary, of course. However, there are common approaches. Typically state laws include:
- a definition of sexual harassment;
- the scope of an employer's liability when sexual harassment occurs;
- what an employer must do, including policy requirements, notices/postings, training programs and complaint procedures; and
- a description of potential penalties.

How is sexual harassment defined? State law will describe what constitutes sexual harassment. For example, sexual harassment may be defined as an invasion of employees' right to privacy. Or, sexual harassment may be defined as unwanted sexual advances or visual, verbal or physical conduct of a sexual nature, encompassing many forms of offensive behavior. The definition may include gender-based harassment of a person of the same sex as the harasser.

In addition to defining sexual harassment, the state law may prohibit retaliation against an employee for filing a complaint or cooperating in a sexual harassment investigation. Sexual harassment may also include harassment on the basis of sexual orientation, or for exercising rights under the law.

What is the employer's potential liability? Generally, state law will specify to what degree employers will be responsible legally for the actions that occur in their workplaces. Typically, an employer is presumed to be liable for an act of sexual harassment by that employer or by any of its employees if:

◆ it happens at work;

◆ the complaining employee tells the employer about it; and

◆ the employer fails to take appropriate action within a reasonable time.

An employer may avoid liability, however, by showing that it took immediate and appropriate corrective action.

WHAT you need to know

In some states, the harasser, as well as any management representative who knew about the harassment and condoned or ratified it, may be held personally liable for damages.

An employer may be liable even if management was not aware of the harassment, which is a hard concept for most managers to embrace. And, an employer may be liable for sexual harassment engaged in by its supervisory employees. In contrast, however, an employer might avoid liability if the harasser is an entry-level employee and if a program to prevent harassment was in place.

Whether the employer had control over the accused harasser and any other legal responsibility that the employer may have had for non-employees will be a factor in the employer's liability.

DON'T miss this

An employer can even be sued for sex discrimination by employees who were "innocent bystanders" if employment opportunities or benefits are granted because of a sexual relationship in the workplace, whether welcome or unwelcome. This could result if other persons were qualified for those employment opportunities or benefits but were denied them because they were granted on the basis of sexual conduct.

What must the employer do? State sexual harassment laws generally describe the actions that an employer should take to prevent harassment, investigate allegations if it occurs, and lessen its impact. Common requirements may include:

◆ **Take action immediately.** An employer is usually directed to take immediate and appropriate action when it knows, or should have known, that sexual harassment has occurred. An employer must take effective action to stop any further harassment and to ameliorate any effects of the harassment.

◆ **Communicate the complaint procedure.** Types of actions employers should take include a complaint procedure with provisions that fully inform complainants of their rights and any obligations to secure those rights, and effectively investigate any complaint.

◆ **Investigate thoroughly.** When required, investigations usually must be immediate, thorough, objective and complete. A determination must be made and the results communicated to the complainant, to the alleged harasser and, as appropriate, to all others directly concerned.

◆ **Provide a prompt remedy.** When harassment is proven, state law may require prompt and effective remedial action. This can include action taken against the harasser and communicated to the complainant. Typically, the employer must take steps to prevent any further harassment, and to remedy any loss experienced by the victim.

◆ **Communicate the policy against harassment.** Other remedial actions may include affirmatively raising the subject, expressing strong disapproval, developing appropriate sanctions, informing employees of their right to raise and how to raise the issue of harassment, and developing methods to sensitize all concerned.

◆ **Document and keep confidential.** There may be guidance concerning how to manage the complaint file, including all information and documents pertinent to a complaint, and requiring that the file be kept confidential.

◆ **Train.** Employers may also be required to educate and provide structured training for all managers in their responsibility for identifying sexual harassment and appropriately dealing with complaints and solving related problems and provide awareness programs for employees.

State law may also require that information on the procedures for filing complaints with enforcement agencies be provided when requested. In some states, employers are not provided with much more guidance than the suggestion that an employer must take all measures that are necessary or suitable for compliance.

Is a policy required? Some states will specify what an employer's policy against sexual harassment must contain. Generally the employer will be required to describe sexual harassment, provide examples of unlawful conduct and set out the consequences for committing sexual harassment. A law mandating a policy will also usually require the employer to provide an internal complaint process. The employer may also have to provide information about state and federal discrimination enforcement agencies.

Some states will provide a model policy and notice form for employers' use. Other states require that the written sexual harassment policy includes information on the illegality of sexual harassment and/or may require the inclusion of the state law definition of sexual harassment, with description and examples.

WHAT you need to know

In addition to specifying what must be contained in sexual harassment policies, states may require other actions, such as a review of policies to be done on a defined timeframe, posting the policy in a specific manner, writing the policy at a specific literacy level, and how the policy must be distributed. States may also require that employers maintain at their business premises records of their sexual harassment policies and make the policy available to enforcement agencies when requested.

Is training required? It is common for states to require that employers conduct sexual harassment training. The state law may define who must be trained and how long the training must be. Typically, training is required for employees, supervisors and managers. It may also be mandatory for all directors. Some states require that new supervisors and managers be trained within a specific timeframe after assuming their duties.

Sexual harassment training is designed to develop an awareness of appropriate rules and policies on the job and knowledge of disciplinary actions against those who sexually harass others. In some states, training must address the seriousness of violations of the employer's sexual harassment policy. Employers may be required to train supervisory personnel about their specific responsibilities in handling sexual harassment and to caution employees against applying peer pressure to discourage harassment victims from using the internal grievance procedure. The content of the training may be prescribed and could include specific steps that employees must take to ensure immediate and appropriate corrective action in addressing sexual harassment complaints.

Some states have established a task force to educate the public, identify the extent of the problem, and develop educational materials, training programs and funding. There may be inexpensive or free resources for employers.

DON'T miss this

What are the posting and notice requirements? States may specify that employers post information and provide notices to employees concerning their rights to a workplace free from sexual harassment. Issues to watch out for include:

◆ A requirement to post a notice in prominent and accessible locations. The actual notice may be specified or the state merely may outline what must be posted.

◆ A requirement to provide information on inquiries and complaints.

◆ Penalties for failure to post the notice, such as a fine.

◆ A requirement that the employer advise employees of their complaint rights through state and federal agencies.

◆ A requirement to periodically advise employees of their rights in writing. For example, an employer may be required to deliver notice with employee paychecks to ensure receipt.

◆ Model rules and question-and-answer statements on sexual harassment. These documents may include information on illegal sexual harassment, employer liability, how sexual harassment can be avoided in the workplace and complaint/grievance procedures.

Penalties. Each state may specify the penalties associated with violations of its sexual harassment law. In some instances, there may be a standard penalty based upon the level of the violation. In other circumstances, there may be several possible penalties, depending upon the number of violations. As a general rule, the party who is found responsible for the harassing behavior is responsible for the payment of attorneys' fees and the costs of the procedure as set by the court.

Typically when fines are levied, the amount of the fine is generally a sum of money that has a relationship to the amount of the damages that the act caused the victim (employee or job applicant) to incur, or the law may specify a flat amount. In other situations, at the court's discretion, the court may order damages and may also order the employer to employ, promote or reinstate the aggrieved employee or applicant in the job, and to cease and desist from such harassment.

The Quiz

1. In recent years, complaints of sexual harassment to the EEOC have:
   a. Decreased.
   b. Increased.
   c. Stayed the same.

2. An employee who joins in with sex jokes ❑ True ❑ False
   or sexual banter in the workplace may be
   a victim of sexual harassment.

3. An employee who consents to a supervisor's ❑ True ❑ False
   sexual advances cannot bring a lawsuit for
   sexual harassment.

4. For the past several months, Tim has regularly told his coworker,
   Walter, that he smells nice and looks good in his work uniform. Tim
   has also made daily comments to Walter about the appearance of
   other men. Walter's coworkers have had similar experiences with
   Tim and regularly tease Walter for having to work alone with him.
   Tim's behavior makes Walter very uncomfortable and nervous. Can
   Tim's conduct be considered sexual harassment?
   a. Yes, because Tim's behavior is unwelcome and gender based,
      and appears to be severe and pervasive.
   b. No, because a man cannot sexually harass another man.
   c. No, because Tim has not touched Walter.

Answer key: 1.b, 2.T, 3.F, 4.a

Employer liability

Introduction.. 66

Liability standards 67

"Alter ego" harassment 67

Supervisor harassment.. 67

Who is a supervisor? 67

Vicarious liability 68

Job action taken—automatic liability 69

No job action—limited defense.. 70

BEST PRACTICES:

Effective complaint procedure saves the day 72

Personal liability 73

Coworker harassment... 73

Knowledge 73

Stopping the harassment 74

Non-employee harassment.. 75

Good faith efforts.. 76

BEST PRACTICES:

Creating an effective anti-discrimination program 76

The Quiz... 78

You receive a telephone call from an attorney who claims to represent a group of African American males that work on an assembly line at one of your company's factories. The attorney states that the workers will be filing a charge of race discrimination with the Equal Employment Opportunity Commission unless steps are immediately taken to stop the racially hostile environment that plagues the factory in which the men work. Further, the attorney warns you that because the harassment involves supervisory personnel, the company faces "vicarious liability." She says that if she discovers that any "tangible actions" have been taken against any of the men, she will certainly see to it that a claim against the company is filed in federal court. You are dumbfounded. To your knowledge, nobody has ever complained about racial harassment at the factory. The company provides annual anti-harassment training and has in place a strong anti-discrimination policy that includes a detailed complaint procedure with several avenues for reporting of harassment. Can the company still be legally responsible if harassment has occurred? What does vicarious liability mean? What is a tangible job action?

Introduction

What actions HR takes to prevent and react to workplace harassment will play a large part in determining whether an employer will be held legally responsible for any harassment that may still occur. To better understand these necessary steps (which are addressed in other chapters of this book), HR must develop a good awareness of when and why an organization might be liable for harassment. Liability refers to the point at which a court or federal agency will hold the employer legally responsible for the harassment and require it to pay financial damages to the victim.

DON'T miss this

A survey by the Society for Human Resources Management (SHRM) found that more than half of responding organizations had been named as a defendant in at least one employment-related lawsuit (1999 Employment Practices Liability Survey).

When a formal charge of harassment is filed with a federal or state agency, or a lawsuit is brought against the organization, one primary issue will be what (if anything) the employer did to prevent or stop the harassment. If HR has taken the necessary steps to eliminate harassment, the employer can generally avoid liability. If the harassment has been eliminated, any lost job benefits have been restored, and preventive measures have been put in place to stop future harassment, the complaint of unlawful harassment will generally be dismissed because of HR's quick action. At the very least, the employer's financial liability will be substantially reduced.

Liability standards

Employers may be held liable for their own acts of harassment ("alter ego" harassment), as well as for harassment committed by:

- ◆ supervisory personnel;
- ◆ employees; and
- ◆ non-employees.

Different standards of liability apply depending upon the status of the harasser. In other words, employers have different responsibilities depending on who engages in harassment. Courts impose the strictest of liability standards on harassment committed by company officials and lesser standards on non-supervisory workers and non-employees.

"Alter Ego" harassment

An employer will be strictly liable for workplace harassment committed by an official of sufficiently high rank to be considered the organization's "proxy" or "alter ego." Strict liability means that the employer will be automatically liable with no defense whatsoever, even if the harassment victim suffered no adverse employment action.

Examples of officials who would be considered a "proxy" or "alter ego" of the organization include:

- ◆ president;
- ◆ owner;
- ◆ partner; and
- ◆ corporate officer.

Supervisor harassment

Who is a supervisor?

A primary issue in establishing an employer's liability for workplace harassment is determining whether the person engaging in the harassment is a supervisory employee. A supervisory employee has been defined by the US Supreme Court as one with "direct or successively higher authority over the victim."

What does this mean? It's not entirely clear, but the EEOC has provided some guidance. Using a fact-specific analysis, the EEOC will determine that an individual qualifies as an employee's "supervisor" if:

1. the individual has authority to undertake or recommend tangible employment decisions affecting the employee; or
2. the individual has authority to direct the employee's daily work activities.

Because someone who has authority over another may not be viewed as a "supervisor" or "manager" in title, it is important that HR consider the particular circumstances rather than the person's job title in determining potential liability. For example, suppose Ashok and Jack are both editors at a publishing company and the manager of the editorial department is Lucinda. Lucinda has asked Ashok to regularly review Jack's work and to make a recommendation as to whether Jack should receive a merit increase. Even if Ashock and Jack have the same job title, Ashok may be viewed as an individual with "supervisory authority" over Jack.

Vicarious liability

If a supervisor engages in sexual or other unlawful harassment of a subordinate or lower-level employee, the employer will be "vicariously liable" if the victim decides to sue.

In 1998, the US Supreme Court announced the vicarious liability standard for sexual harassment by a supervisor with authority over the victim. Although the Court's holding pertained only to sexual harassment, the EEOC and several federal appeals courts have taken the position that the vicarious liability standard applies to harassment claims based on any protected class.

Understanding vicarious liability. Vicarious liability means that an organization will be *automatically* liable for the wrongdoing of others, regardless of fault. The employer will be treated as if it engaged in the wrongdoing itself. To say that an employer is vicariously liable for a supervisor's actions means that it is liable even if no members of HR or management knew about the harassment.

Job action taken—automatic liability

If a supervisor's harassment included the taking of a "tangible employment action" against the victim, the employer will have no defense to charges of unlawful harassment whatsoever.

What is a tangible job action? The US Supreme Court has stated that a tangible employment action occurs when there is:

◆ a significant change in employment status—such as hiring, firing, failing to promote, or reassigning with significantly different responsibilities; or

◆ a decision causing a significant change in benefits—such as a significant reduction in pay or loss of health benefits.

A direct monetary loss is not necessary in order for conduct to constitute a tangible job action. Rather, the loss of significant job benefits or characteristics—such as the loss of resources necessary for an employee to do his or her job—may constitute a tangible job action.

Worst case scenario

Ben works as a supervisor in an insurance company. He makes sexual overtures towards Sonya, a saleswoman. When Sonya rejects his advances, Ben eliminates her private office, dismisses her secretary, causes her files to disappear, and reassigns her work in a manner that results in a loss of pay.

Solution. Ben is engaging in inappropriate behavior and he's putting the organization at extreme risk for liability. In a case with similar facts, a court held the employer strictly liable for the harassment because tangible job actions were taken against the victim. In deciding whether a tangible job action has occurred, don't only focus on obvious actions—such as a termination or demotion. Although direct economic harm is an important indicator of a tangible adverse employment action, if a supervisor's conduct substantially decreases an employee's earning potential and causes significant disruption in his or her working conditions, a tangible adverse employment action may be found.

Consider the African American employees who have hired an attorney to represent them concerning their claims of racial harassment in the workplace. To determine whether your organization may be at risk for vicarious liability, HR (with the help of legal counsel) must find out who has supervisory authority over these individuals and investigate whether any of the supervisory personnel have engaged in potentially harassing behavior. It is also important to review the job records of the complaining employees to see whether any negative employment actions have been taken against them. If they have, investigate the reasons behind the decisions to make sure they were legitimate. It is important to act as quickly as possible to avoid—or at least limit—the organization's liability.

No job action–limited defense

If a manager or supervisor engages in unlawful harassment, but the victim does not suffer a tangible employment action, the employer may be able to defend itself from liability and/or damages if the victim sues. The employer will be required to prove two things:

1. that the employer exercised reasonable care to prevent and correct promptly harassing behavior, and
2. that the victim unreasonably failed to take advantage of any preventive or corrective opportunities provided by the employer or to avoid harm otherwise.

The employer's reasonable care. What will be considered "reasonable care" to prevent harassment will depend upon the particular employment circumstances. However, reasonableness will generally require an employer to have in place an anti-harassment policy with an effective complaint procedure that allows an employee to bypass his or her supervisor in reporting workplace harassment. Also important to the reasonableness inquiry is whether managers and supervisors are trained in preventing workplace harassment and monitored for EEO-compliance.

Reasonable care also requires immediate and appropriate corrective action by the employer once workplace harassment is known. Remedial measures should be designed to stop the harassment, correct its effects on the employee and ensure that the harassment does not continue to occur.

> The remedial measures need not be those that the employee requests or prefers, as long as they are effective.

WHAT you need to know

The employee's reasonable care. An employer may be able to show that the employee acted unreasonably if he or she failed to bring harassment to the attention of HR. Unless it would be unreasonable to do so, an employee must use the employer's complaint procedure or otherwise bring workplace harassment to the employer's attention. The employee's failure to use a complaint procedure that was communicated and reasonably designed will normally satisfy a court that the employee acted unreasonably.

However, there are some situations that may make it reasonable for an employee not to complain. These circumstances include:

◆ if the employee had reason to believe that there was a risk of retaliation;

◆ if there were obstacles to bringing a complaint; or

◆ if the complaint mechanism was not effective.

One way that the EEOC recommends for HR to increase employee confidence in the complaint process is to release general information to employees about corrective and disciplinary measures undertaken by the organization to stop harassment. However, to avoid a possible defamation claim by the alleged harasser, employers should not release any specific information. So what's an HR professional to do? It is best to consult legal counsel on this matter (see Chapter 9 for more information concerning potential defamation claims).

DON'T miss this

Risk of retaliation. An employee who reasonably fears retaliation will not be required to use an organization's complaint procedure to report harassment. To assure employees that such a fear is unreasonable, the employer must clearly communicate and enforce a policy that no employee will be retaliated against for complaining of harassment or assisting in an investigation.

Obstacles to complaints. Some examples of obstacles to bringing a complaint include undue expense by a complaining employee, designating inaccessible officials to accept complaints, or putting requirements on making a complaint that are unnecessarily intimidating or burdensome. The EEOC will not find an employee's failure to participate in a mandatory mediation or other alternative dispute resolution policy to be unreasonable.

Ineffective complaint mechanism. An employee might reasonably believe that complaining would be ineffective if the organization's complaint procedure requires the employee to first report the harassment to the harassing supervisor. An employee could also reasonably believe reporting harassment would be futile if the employer has a history of failing to stop known harassment.

A⁺ *Best Practices*

Effective complaint procedure saves the day

An employer avoided liability because there was no evidence that it knew or should have known that a male supervisor was sexually harassing a female employee in a retail store. The employee sued the employer, claiming that during her 14-month tenure, a male supervisor harassed her daily with remarks like "do you scream?" and "you need a man in your bed."

The employee admitted that she was aware of the employer's sexual harassment policy and its procedures for reporting harassment. However, she never complained about being harassed until after she quit her job. Further, the company's director of human resources (one of the corporate officers to whom harassment complaints were to be made), visited the store about twice a week and never witnessed any harassment or heard a complaint from the employee about being harassed. A court decided that the employer could not be held liable if it had no reason to know about the alleged harassment.

Personal liability

Some courts allow a victim of harassment to sue the harasser directly. That means a supervisor who harasses somebody may wind up in court defending him or herself, paying high attorneys' fees and if found guilty, a large sum of money out of his or her own pocket.

Courts are divided over whether managers and supervisors can be held personally liable for unlawful harassment that violates federal law. But even if they aren't held personally responsible under federal law, managers and supervisors may still be liable if their harassing behavior is unlawful for other reasons (such as assault or battery), or if the conduct takes place in a state that has an anti-discrimination law that provides for personal liability.

DON'T miss this

Coworker harassment

An employer will be liable for the actions of coworkers that create a hostile work environment. Unlike harassment by company officials, supervisors or managers, employers will not be automatically responsible for such harassment. Rather, the EEOC and courts will ask two basic questions when determining whether an organization is liable for harassment by coworkers:

◆ Did the employer know or should it have known that harassment was taking place?

◆ Did the employer take any action to stop the harassment?

Knowledge

An employer's knowledge may come from a complaint made to HR, firsthand observation by supervisory personnel, or a formal charge of harassment to the EEOC.

An employer will be assumed to know about harassment that is openly practiced in the workplace or is well known among employees. An example would be a nude pin-up calendar and sexually explicit cartoons posted in a common work area.

WHAT you need to know

Failure to report. There is no requirement that a victim report workplace harassment. Evidence that the conduct was reported is just *one* means of establishing employer knowledge. A victim's failure to report the conduct does not automatically preclude a finding that the employer knew or had reason to know about workplace harassment.

That being said, an employer that has distributed a bias-free policy that clearly defines the steps an employee must take to report workplace harassment may be deemed *not* to have notice if a victimized employee fails to report the harassment.

Stopping the harassment

Once an employer is aware of workplace harassment, it will be liable unless it takes action that is reasonably likely to end the harassing conduct. Generally, employers are held to standards that require:

◆ prompt action;
◆ consideration of reassignment; and
◆ follow up.

> **Example:** *Tamika believed that her coworker, George, was sexually harassing her because he repeatedly asked her to go out on a date with him. Tamika mentioned the situation to a supervisor. The supervisor told HR, and the company investigated thoroughly. Although it was determined that the evidence concerning sexual harassment was inconclusive, HR transferred George to another area where he would not have any contact with Tamika. The company also allowed her to work at home until the transfer was completed. In a case with similar facts, a court found that the employer's actions were reasonable because they stopped the harassing conduct promptly.*

Prompt action. If harassment is occurring in the workplace, HR must do more than take remedial action. The action taken must be prompt, effective and reasonably calculated to end the harassment.

Reassignments. In many cases, employers consider reassigning the alleged harasser and/or the victim to different work areas so that they no longer work together. Any such transfer has to be handled cautiously, especially if the victim is to be transferred.

Since federal law prohibits adverse employment actions against an employee who opposes discrimination, the employer must ensure that the new position is substantially equal to the previous position held by the employee and that the employee voluntarily consents to the transfer. For more information on reassignments, see Chapter 10.

> **Example:** *A court determined that a company's choice to reassign a sexual harassment victim, rather than moving or firing the harasser, was a satisfactory response. Here, the harassed employee had been assigned only temporarily to work under the guilty foreman. In addition to separating the two people, management reprimanded the foreman, told him to stay away from the female employee and later denied him a promotion and merit increase.*

Follow up. After workplace harassment has occurred and management has taken the appropriate action, HR should follow up with the victim and any witnesses to ensure that the harassment has stopped and that no retaliation is taking place. In addition to protecting the victim from future harassment, this also demonstrates HR's support of the victim for reporting the incident.

Non-employee harassment

An employer can also be held responsible for unlawful harassment by third parties in the workplace, such as customers, sales representatives, subcontractors, repair workers or independent contractors.

As with coworkers, the courts will ask whether the employer knew or should have known about the harassment. If the employer has control over the situation to stop the improper conduct by the third party, immediate corrective action must be taken if feasible.

WHAT you need to know

Good faith efforts

Another issue of liability concerns that of punitive damages. Punitive damages are awarded by the court to punish an employer for its unlawful actions, such as for harassment or discrimination. These damages, if awarded to the victim, are in addition to compensatory damages. Compensatory damages are meant to compensate the victim for specific losses, such as lost pay and emotional suffering.

An employer may be able to escape punitive damages liability if it can show that a manager's discriminatory or harassing employment actions were contrary to the employer's "good faith efforts" to comply with the law, according the US Supreme Court. Although the Court has not elaborated on what constitutes "good faith," it has granted HR the ability to take control over an organization's fate in the punitive damages arena. A fundamental reevaluation of company strategy, vision, mission and values is called for, Jackson Lewis attorneys Lynn Outwater and Michael J. Lotito told attendees at the 1999 meeting of the Society for Human Resources Management.

Best Practices

Creating an effective anti-discrimination program

Lynn Outwater and Michael Lotito suggest taking these key actions:

Stay current. Demonstrating a good faith attempt to understand employer obligations under employment laws requires continual monitoring of federal and state requirements.

Review and revise the bias-free policy. Does the policy clearly define acceptable workplace behavior? The policy should set a standard of zero tolerance of workplace harassment and extend to all aspects of the employment relationship.

Review any complaint procedures. Make multiple complaint options available—multiple channels, reporting relationships, even a hotline, if possible. Affirm the organization's commitment to investigate complaints and take appropriate action against anyone who violates the policy.

Communicate the policy effectively and repeatedly. Use corporate intranets, recruiting literature, application forms, handbooks, training, employee orientation, annual reports and other appropriate forums, including face-to-face discussion.

Train managers and supervisors about discriminatory practices. Make sure they know who is covered, what types of behavior to avoid and what to do if they observe or hear complaints of discriminatory conduct. Train at least annually and as part of new employee orientation.

Monitor all employment actions for compliance. This includes hiring, discipline, promotion, demotion, layoffs, termination, wage and salary actions, transfers and training. Do policies also protect against retaliation? Is the zero-tolerance policy reflected in the organization's day-to-day actions?

Reevaluate supervisory selection and performance appraisal procedures. Is compliance with and support of the organization's bias-free position as important as "making the numbers" or "getting the job done?" If not, what message is the organization really sending?

Measure the efforts. Do the bias-free policies, complaint procedures, communication vehicles, training methods, day-to-day activities, supervisory selection and performance appraisal systems actually work? How well are they documented? If harassment is found, is immediate action taken to remedy it? What follow-up procedures are taken?

The Quiz

1. An employer will not be liable for workplace ❑ True ❑ False
   harassment committed by managers or
   supervisors as long as it is not aware of the conduct.

2. An individual will be considered an employee's "supervisor" if:
   a. The individual has authority to undertake or recommend tangible
      employment decisions affecting the employee.
   b. The individual has authority to direct the employee's daily
      work activities.
   c. Either choice a or b.
   d. Neither choice a or b.

3. If a supervisor's harassment includes taking ❑ True ❑ False
   a tangible employment action against the victim,
   the employer will be able to defend itself by
   showing that it acted reasonably.

4. What does it mean for an employer to be "vicariously liable" for a
   supervisor's harassment?
   a. The employer is liable even if no members of HR or manage-
      ment knew about the harassment.
   b. The employer is liable only if the victim was fired.
   c. The employer is liable only if the victim reported the harassment.
   d. None of the above.

5. An employer will be assumed to know ❑ True ❑ False
   about coworker harassment that is openly
   practiced in the workplace or is well known
   among employees.

Answer key: 1.F, 2.c, 3.F, 4.a, 5.T.

Chapter

6

Policy creation
and communication

Why have a policy?... 80

Key provisions 80

    Harassment prohibition 81

    Complaint procedure... 83

    BEST PRACTICES: 24-hour hot line encourages
        victims to come forward 85

    Protection from retaliation 88

    Prompt investigation 89

    Confidentiality... 90

    Disciplining the offender.. 90

    BEST PRACTICES: Sample equal employment
        opportunity policy 91

Communicating the policy 93

    Distribute and post.. 93

    Train 94

    Get acknowledgment 94

    BEST PRACTICES: Communicating the policy
        saved a company at trial 95

The Quiz... 96

*Irum, a Muslim employee who has resigned from your organi-
zation, meets with you for her exit interview. When asked why
she decided to resign, Irum states, "I had no other choice." You
probe further and Irum eventually tells you that she is leaving
because she was unhappy working in an environment where
others ridiculed her dress and ethnic background. Irum is visibly
upset, but says that she has no intention of taking legal action
since she just wants to put this "terrible" experience behind her.
You are stunned and ask Irum if she ever reported the behavior*

to management. Irum replies that she was afraid to complain since she once overheard her supervisor make an offensive comment about Muslims in America.

After Irum leaves the office, you meet with your HR counterparts and plan an immediate investigation into Irum's complaints to determine whether ethnic harassment is occurring in your organization. You also review your EEO policy, which states that the company will not tolerate unlawful discrimination. The policy does not prohibit retaliation and advises employees to report discrimination to their immediate supervisors. Is the policy sufficient? Should you revise the policy to help ensure another situation like Irum's doesn't slip through the cracks? What kind of complaint procedure should you have in place?

Why have a policy?

A policy that prohibits harassment and discrimination in the workplace is an integral part of any organization's efforts to create a bias-free workplace. The creation and distribution of an adequate policy is one of the most crucial steps that HR can take to prevent workplace harassment and to avoid liability should unlawful behavior occur. A company that does not establish and distribute a clear policy against workplace harassment—and provide a reasonable avenue for victims to complain to someone with authority to investigate and remedy the problem—may be held liable for unlawful harassment regardless of whether it knew of the conduct.

It is best to have a policy in place that bans more than unlawful harassment and discrimination. In order to ensure a work environment that is free from harassment and any other form of discrimination, put in place a policy that encourages *respect* in the workplace. And make sure that the policy is written so that all employees can understand it.

Key provisions

HR may choose to call the policy an "EEO" policy, a "bias-free" policy, an "anti-harassment" policy or something else. Regardless of what you call it, there are several provisions that you should include in your policy against discrimination and harassment. The most important provisions are:

- ◆ A clear prohibition against harassment and discrimination.
- ◆ An effective procedure for reporting harassment or other inappropriate behavior.
- ◆ A clear prohibition against retaliation.
- ◆ A description of the investigation process.
- ◆ Confidentiality expectations.
- ◆ An explanation of discipline.

There are several examples in this Chapter of language you may want to use in your policy against discrimination and harassment, as well as a sample EEO policy. Before adopting a particular bias-free policy, including using any of the sample language in this Chapter, you'll have to ensure that all applicable laws are considered. If in doubt, it's advisable that you consult competent counsel on that issue. Also make sure that your policy concerning discrimination and harassment is consistent with all other policies and procedures.

DON'T
miss
this

Harassment prohibition

The bias-free policy should begin with an anti-discrimination statement telling employees that the organization is committed to equal opportunity for all employees, and listing the protected classes established under federal law:

- ◆ Race
- ◆ Color
- ◆ Religion
- ◆ National origin
- ◆ Citizenship
- ◆ Disability
- ◆ Age
- ◆ Sex
- ◆ Veterans' status

If applicable, the policy should also include a similar statement that prohibits any discrimination against persons in those characteristics protected by state law—such as discrimination based on sexual orientation, marital or family status, arrest or criminal record, personal appearance, HIV/AIDS, and sickle-cell or genetic traits.

WHAT you need to know

To make clear the organization's commitment, include a statement that the policy applies to *all* of the organization's policies and procedures concerning recruitment and hiring, compensation, benefits, training, discipline, termination and all other terms and conditions of employment. If a separate sexual harassment policy is in place, include a reference to it. If required by the employer's status as a federal contractor or its receipt of federal funds, include an affirmative action statement.

Respect is key. To make sure that workers don't get into a guessing game over what is technically unlawful behavior and what is not, insist that people treat each other with respect. Explain that behavior which does not rise to the level of unlawful activity, but that a reasonable person would find offensive and inappropriate for the workplace, violates the organization's policy against inappropriate behavior. Advise workers to use common sense in their interactions with coworkers, managers and persons outside the organization.

✓ *Checklist*

Examples of harassing conduct

Help employees understand the types of behavior that are inappropriate for the workplace by including examples of potentially harassing conduct. Some examples could be:

☐ Asking unwelcome questions or making unwelcome comments about another person's sexual activities, dating, personal or intimate relationships, or appearance (for example, commenting on the attractiveness of males or females in the workplace).

☐ Making comments about a person's protected group that demean or show hostility to a person because of his or her membership in the protected class (for example, referring to older workers as "snow caps" or calling an employee with schizophrenia a "nut case").

☐ Displaying objects or pictures that are sexually suggestive or that demean or show hostility to a person because of the

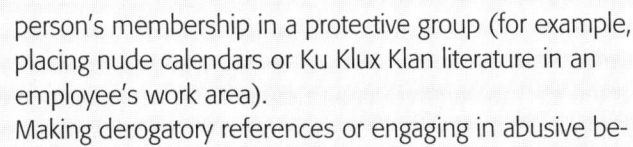

person's membership in a protective group (for example, placing nude calendars or Ku Klux Klan literature in an employee's work area).

☐ Making derogatory references or engaging in abusive behavior that is directed at an employee because of his or her membership in a protected group (for example, name-calling and racial slurs).

Define sexual harassment. The bias-free policy should specifically prohibit sexual harassment and other inappropriate behavior. Because it is so often misunderstood, it is a good idea to provide a definition of sexual harassment. Make clear that no employee—either male or female—should be subject to unwelcome verbal or physical conduct that is sexual in nature or that shows hostility to the employee because of the employee's gender.

For example, state that:

Sexual harassment does not refer to occasional compliments of a socially acceptable nature. It refers to behavior that is not welcome, that is personally offensive, that hurts morale, and that, therefore, interferes with work effectiveness. Sexual harassment includes, but is not limited to, making sexual advances or requests for sexual favors, as well as other forms of verbal or physical conduct that show hostility toward an employee because of the employee's gender, where either:

◆ *submission to the conduct is an explicit or implicit condition of employment; or*

◆ *submission to or rejection of the conduct is used as a basis for employment decisions; or*

◆ *the conduct has the purpose or effect of substantially interfering with work performance or creates an intimidating or offensive work environment.*

Complaint procedure

Just as important as the employer's stance against workplace harassment and discrimination is the mechanism it has in place for ensuring that such behavior does not occur. Workers must know how to bring their concerns about workplace discrimination and harassment to someone's attention.

WHAT you need to know

Even if a complaint procedure is in place, HR must still investigate and stop harassment that becomes apparent through its own observation, or the observations of managers and supervisors. Remember that employees can file an EEOC harassment charge without using the complaint procedure.

Why is a complaint procedure important? How are employees going to know how to respond if their organization has no specific procedures for dealing with harassment? If no effective complaint procedure is in place, it is reasonable for employees to believe that harassment will be ignored, tolerated or even condoned by management. That's the first reason a complaint procedure is important.

Additionally, when a supervisor engages in sexual or other unlawful harassment, the employer likely will be automatically liable if no policy against harassment has been established and if there is no system to allow victims to complain to someone with authority to investigate and remedy the problem. And even if the harasser is a coworker or nonemployee, the employer may still be liable because it "should have known" of the harassment, and did not know only because the employee had no effective means to report it.

On the other hand, an effective complaint procedure that encourages employees to complain about sexual or other unlawful harassment puts the employer in a stronger position to defend against a harassment claim. In the case of harassment by a manager or supervisor, the employer may be able to escape otherwise automatic liability. And, if a complaining employee has no legitimate reason for failing to use the complaint procedure, his or her credibility may be damaged. It is also more difficult to claim that harassment forced an employee to quit the job if the employee did not use an effective complaint procedure before quitting.

Effective doesn't necessarily mean "formal." Small businesses do not necessarily have to implement a formal complaint process in order to protect themselves from liability, according to the EEOC. In many cases, informal mechanisms to prevent and correct harassment should suffice. It is important, however, for the employer to effectively communicate both the prohibition against harassment and its effective complaint procedure to all employees regularly at staff meetings.

Remember Irum, who said that she didn't complain because her supervisor had himself made comments about her ethnicity that she found inappropriate? If it turns out that Irum was in fact a victim of ethnic harassment, the organization could have trouble claiming that she should have complained about the conduct if there was not an effective complaint procedure in place with several avenues for complaint.

How can HR establish an effective reporting mechanism? For one, make sure the policy urges employees to come forward and report incidents of improper workplace behavior as soon as they happen. Next, outline a procedure for employees to make complaints about harassment and discrimination. Make sure the avenues of complaint are accessible. For example, if you have a 24-hour workforce, make sure complaints may be brought 24 hours a day.

Best Practices
24-hour hot line encourages victims to come forward

A crucial component of one manufacturing company's sexual harassment program is its 24-hour employee hot line. The hot line, which started out as a way for workers to report rape, gives employees the opportunity to get help confidentially.

How does it work? A staff member answers the hot line for a week at a time. The hot line goes first into an answering service that beeps the staff person as soon as there is a call.

All hot line staff who are assigned for a particular week carry beepers 24 hours a day. As soon as the individual's beeper goes off—no matter what time of the day or night—he or she contacts the answering service. Responding to the call is that individual's number one priority.

Staff members are advocates as well as counselors. For example, sometimes an employee needs help sorting out exactly what he or she is experiencing. The counselor focuses on providing the caller with options, explaining to the caller what the process is and what decisions he or she might have to make as part of the process. Sometimes a caller simply wants to talk the problem out. In a case like this, the counselor provides therapeutic value by listening.

The counselor may explain to the caller that while the individual has the option of trying to deal with the offender herself, the caller may bring the complaint to the affirmative action officer, HR or a line manager. The caller may even ask the counselor to accompany her or him. The counselor also acts in an advisory capacity. For example, he or she may make recommendations to the department head or HR or may assist in the investigation.

Be sure to provide several avenues for an employee to report harassment so that the employee can bypass his or her supervisor, who might be the alleged harasser. If possible, it is a good idea to designate both males and females as persons to report to because an employee might feel more comfortable reporting harassing behavior to someone of the same sex. Also include the name and phone number of the department that maintains and monitors the policy and who is responsible for responding to questions and concerns.

It is also a good idea to state in the policy that supervisory personnel are required to immediately report suspected sexual or other unlawful harassment. Supervisors are considered agents of the organization and as such should understand their responsibility for protecting it. State that failure to report harassment will result in appropriate discipline, which may include termination.

Worst case scenario

A junior college was unable to defend itself against a sexual harassment lawsuit because its anti-harassment policy was inadequate. In this case, a night shift employee claimed that her supervisor exposed himself to her and requested oral sex in return for giving her Fridays off with pay. After an unsuccessful attempt to file a complaint with her neighborhood police department, the employee filed a complaint with the Tulsa Police Department. She did not file a formal complaint with the campus police, but a campus police supervisor became aware of the incident the morning after it occurred. That campus police supervisor chose not to report the incident to his superiors or to campus administrators. Instead, he instructed a subordinate to gather information from the accused harasser and took no further action based on the investigation.

Although the college had a sexual harassment policy in place that provided a way for employees to bypass their supervisor and report harassment to the Director of Personnel, the director's office was located in a separate facility and was not accessible during evening hours or on weekends. The policy also did not:

◆ define what constituted a formal complaint;
◆ explain the responsibility of college managers to report sexual harassment incidents; or
◆ require campus police to report such incidents to college administrators.

Solution. If workers are located at more than one facility, it may be necessary to designate persons at each facility to accept complaints of workplace harassment, or to provide a telephone hot line. HR must also make sure that all persons charged with authority for reporting harassment understand the importance that they do so immediately.

Who receives harassment complaints? You know that HR needs to designate and train several persons to receive complaints of harassment, but who should be chosen? These persons may include the employee's supervisor or manager, the head of human resources, the EEO officer or someone else designated in the organization. Just remember that there must always be an alternative path for reporting incidents of harassment in case the alleged harasser is the person to whom the complaint would otherwise be made.

✓ Checklist

Selecting persons to receive complaints

When deciding who should receive complaints, there are several considerations:

☐ Are the designated representatives reasonably available when employees are working, including evening and weekend shifts?

☐ Is each representative someone to whom employees would feel comfortable bringing a complaint?

☐ Is each representative sufficiently trained to respond effectively to complaints of workplace harassment?

☐ Is the representative able to maintain privacy and confidentiality?

☐ Where an organization has multiple locations, but does not maintain an HR person at each site, is there an appropriate officer or management employee available?

Protection from retaliation

HR must make sure that all communications regarding the organization's bias-free policy stress that employees will not be retaliated against for bringing a complaint of harassment. Nor will there be any retaliation for providing support as a witness in a harassment investigation. State in your policy that no one reporting inappropriate discriminatory conduct will be disciplined or retaliated against, even if a report made in good faith is later determined to be unfounded.

Include in your prohibition against retaliation protection for any employees who assist in investigating complaints of improper conduct. Make clear that employees who engage in retaliatory conduct are subject to discipline up to and including termination.

Federal law prohibits retaliation against an employee because he or she has opposed discriminatory practices by making a complaint or participating in an investigation. To reduce the risk of retaliation claims, HR should act carefully before making any employment decision that could be perceived as having a negative effect on someone who has complained about harassment or participated in the investigation of a harassment complaint.

WHAT you need to know

Think back to Irum, who was afraid that she would be retaliated against if she complained about what she perceived to be an ethnically hostile work environment. Irum needed reassurances from the organization that her complaint would be taken seriously *and* that she would be protected from retaliation. Because she didn't get such reassurances, she chose to remain silent and find another job. She could have chosen to bring her complaint to an outside agency, like the EEOC, and the organization could have not only faced losing a valuable employee, but also the expense and disruption of a possible lawsuit.

Prompt investigation

A statement in the bias-free policy about the investigation process is a good idea. For example, HR may choose to say that once a complaint of workplace harassment is made and the employer is aware of the problem, an immediate internal investigation will be conducted according to the employer's policy.

Communicate that the goal of the investigation will be to gather all facts so that management can determine whether inappropriate conduct has occurred. Assure that the facts will be kept confidential under a strict "need to know" basis as much as possible.

HR may also want to explain what will happen once the investigation is complete. It is probably not a good idea to promise disclosure of full details. Rather, state that the parties will be informed of the results and if corrective action was taken. Caution that the person who made the complaint usually will not be told about the particulars of the disciplinary actions being taken, other than that the employer has acted appropriately. Encourage workers who are involved in a harassment investigation to immediately let management know if there are any further problems.

Confidentiality

Don't promise what you can't deliver. It is best to assure confidentiality without promising absolute secrecy. Assure only that all complaints will be handled as confidentially as possible. State that once an investigation has begun, the facts will be kept under a strict "need to know" basis as much as possible. Advise that all people involved in the harassment—including the complainant, the accused and witnesses—will be asked to keep investigatory discussions strictly confidential.

✓ Checklist

Persons with a "need to know"

People who would likely need to be apprised about the facts of a harassment investigation include:

☐ persons investigating the complaint;
☐ the person accused of harassment;
☐ witnesses;
☐ persons involved in making decisions based on the outcome of the investigation; and
☐ any other management-level persons who have a legitimate need to know.

Disciplining the offender

Many experts recommend that the bias-free policy include a statement of what the organization will do if, following an investigation, harassment is found to have occurred. This means setting forth the disciplinary measures that may be taken against anyone who is found to have violated the policy.

For example, advise the workforce that a supervisor or employee who is found responsible for harassment will be disciplined, and that the degree of the discipline will reflect the severity of the conduct and who engages in the conduct. State that discipline can include oral or written warnings, reprimands, demotion, suspension and probation. If the conduct is very offensive or if the harassee's ability to perform is very impaired, explain that discharge may be the only alternative. Also, be clear that if the harasser is a supervisor, the most severe penalty—discharge—may be necessary. HR may also want to include a statement that all actions taken as a result of violating the policy will be consistent and timely.

Best Practices

Sample equal employment opportunity policy

One of [Organization]'s fundamental principles is Equal Employment Opportunity. Employment at [Organization] is based upon abilities and qualifications, without discrimination because of race, color, religion, gender, sex, national origin, age, disability, veterans' status or any other status or condition that is protected by applicable state law.

Discriminatory conduct is any form of inappropriate behavior that undermines the employment relationship or that adversely affects an employee's ability to perform his or job. Discriminatory conduct includes harassment, which consists of verbal or physical conduct that denigrates or shows hostility toward an employee because of the employee's race, color, religion, gender, sex, national origin, age, disability, veterans' status or any other protected category. Sexual harassment is one form of inappropriate discriminatory conduct.

Employer's responsibility. [Organization] will recruit, hire, train and promote persons in a nondiscriminatory manner. Decisions will be made based upon skills, abilities and merit. In addition, all compensation, benefit, training, discipline programs and procedures and any other terms and conditions of employment will be administered in a nondiscriminatory manner. [Organization] values diversity.

[Organization] wants you to have a work environment free of discrimination by management personnel, by your coworkers and by others with whom you must interact in the course of your work as a [Organization] employee.

[Organization] management at all levels is responsible for preventing discrimination in the workplace, for taking immediate corrective action to stop discrimination in the workplace and for promptly investigating any allegation of work-related discrimination

Employee respect. [Organization]'s policy against discrimination and harassment requires that employees treat each other with respect. Behavior that a reasonable person would consider offensive and inappropriate in the workplace, even if it does not rise to the level of unlawful conduct, violates the respect rule. Courtesy and common sense should guide interactions with coworkers, managers and customers. Violations of the respect rule must be reported, using the complaint procedure outlined below.

Complaint procedure. If you experience or witness discrimination or harassment in the workplace, report it immediately to Human Resources, the department that has responsibility for maintaining and monitoring this policy. All questions and concerns about the equal employment opportunity policy should be directed to Human Resources. You may also report discrimination or violations of the respect rule to your leader or any other member of [Organization] management. Leaders must immediately inform Human Resources of any complaints received. A leader who has not received a complaint but who suspects conduct that might violate this policy must immediately inform Human Resources, regardless of how the leader became aware of the conduct.

All allegations of discrimination will be quickly investigated. To the extent possible, your confidentiality and that of any witnesses and the alleged discriminator will be protected against unnecessary disclosure. When the investigation is completed, you will be informed of the outcome of that investigation.

Retaliation prohibited. [Organization] will not permit any employment-based retaliation against anyone who brings a complaint of discrimination or who speaks as a witness in the investigation of a complaint of discrimination.

Training. All [Organization] management personnel will participate in antidiscrimination training. In addition, all employees will participate in a workshop about discrimination upon beginning work at [Organization] and, at least _____ while you remain a [Organization] employee.

Communication of policy. [Organization]'s equal employment opportunity policy is posted in several conspicuous locations in the workplace. You will also receive a copy of [Organization 's] antidiscrimination policy when you begin working for [Organization]. If at any time you would like another copy of that policy, please contact _____ . If [Organization] should amend or modify its antidiscrimination policy, you will receive an individual copy of the amended or modified policy.

Penalties. Discrimination will not be tolerated at [Organization]. Persons engaging in discriminatory behavior will be subject to disciplinary action, up to and including dismissal.

Communicating the policy

Obviously, the best policy will do no good if nobody knows about it. Therefore, it is just as important that HR communicates the bias-free policy as it is that HR creates it.

Distribute and post

The policy should be distributed to all new employees at orientation. It is best that HR also redistribute the policy on a regular basis. This serves as a way to remind employees periodically of the organization's position against harassment and discrimination. One method would be to include the policy in the envelope with the employee's paycheck on an annual basis.

HR should also post the policy in central locations, where possible, and incorporate it into employee handbooks. If the workforce is on-line, post the policy electronically. Whether the policy is posted on the employer's premises or on-line, HR should periodically check that it is current.

DON'T miss this

Employers that hire workers who are unfamiliar with English may encounter specialized problems. HR must ensure that there are trusted staff members who will see to it that the bias-free policy is correctly translated into the required language. The translated policy should be carefully edited for grammatical correctness and readability for your non-English-speaking workforce. It is also important that bilingual personnel be available to help ensure optimal communication of the policy.

Train

Train all employees and supervisory staff on the policy to make sure that they understand their rights and responsibilities. Discuss and explain the policy during group meetings. Managers and supervisors should receive specific training to enforce the policy and to be sensitive to improper conduct. Further, supervisory staff should be trained to take appropriate actions. Keep records of attendance at training sessions. Training is discussed further in Chapter 7.

Get acknowledgment

It is very important that HR document the employer's efforts to prevent and eliminate harassment in the workplace. To that end, HR should require workers to sign a form acknowledging that they have received and read the organization's bias-free policy, and promising that they will abide by the rules contained in it. That way, if there is ever a dispute concerning whether an employee knew about the policy and complaint procedure, HR can pull out the acknowledgment form.

⬥ *Best Practices*

Communicating the policy saved a company at trial

An automotive parts retailer was able successfully to defend itself against a sexual harassment lawsuit because it was able to prove that it provided its employees with a policy that included multiple complaint mechanisms. The employee who brought the lawsuit had never complained internally about the alleged harassment. She claimed to have never seen the sexual harassment policy. Her argument lost at court, however, since the retailer was able to demonstrate that she:

◆ received a copy of the policy;

◆ was required as a condition of employment to read and comply with the terms of the policy; and

◆ signed a form acknowledging that she received the policy.

The court determined that the retailer exercised reasonable care to prevent sexual harassment. Its anti-harassment policy provided multiple mechanisms for the prompt resolution of complaints, the policy was distributed to employees, and regular training sessions on sexual harassment were conducted. Since the employee failed utilize *any* of the retailer's complaint mechanisms, the retailer's actions—doing nothing beyond its reasonable attempts to prevent sexual harassment—were enough to prove that it acted reasonably to prevent and respond to the harassment.

❓ *The Quiz*

1. An organization's bias-free policy should include:
   a. A clear prohibition against harassment and discrimination.
   b. A procedure for reporting inappropriate conduct.
   c. A clear prohibition against retaliation.
   d. All of the above.

2. How many persons should be designated in an organization's policy to accept complaints of workplace harassment?
   a. One person.
   b. More than one person, so that the employee can bypass the alleged harasser.
   c. It depends on the composition of the workforce.
   d. Choices b and c.

3. It is best to promise employees that all complaints of workplace harassment will be kept strictly confidential.   ❑ True   ❑ False

4. Workers should be required to sign a form acknowledging that they have received and read the bias-free policy and agree to abide by its terms.   ❑ True   ❑ False

Answer key: 1.d, 2.d, 3.F, 4.T

Anti-harassment training

Training overview 98

    Legal reasons to train 99

    BEST PRACTICES: PPG Industries
        receives high marks from the EEOC 99

    Who to train 100

    When to train 101

    Training components 101

Communicating the policy 102

Explaining harassment 104

    Make it understandable 104

    BEST PRACTICES: Training tools help reinforce learning.... 105

    BEST PRACTICES: Training focuses
        on creating a respectful workplace 107

Manager and supervisor training 108

    Avoiding supervisory harassment 108

    Monitoring the workplace 109

    Responding to a complaint 109

Documenting training efforts 110

Evaluation 111

The Quiz 113

As part of your organization's bias-free workplace efforts, you have developed and distributed a clear policy against workplace harassment that provides several avenues for victims to complain. The policy encourages potential victims to come forward and makes clear that retaliation will not be tolerated. You have also set up an internal procedure for investigating harassment and have adopted disciplinary measures to follow in the event that the policy is violated. But beyond passing out the policy and posting it on your organization's internal

Web site, you have not provided any specific training to your employees about workplace harassment or the policy against it. You trained your upper-level managers about sexual harassment, but that was three years ago. You decide its time to audit your training efforts. Should you train your employees or just your supervisory personnel? What do they need to know about workplace harassment?

Training overview

As HR professionals know, what employers don't do to combat workplace harassment can come back to haunt them in the form of lost productivity, a disruptive workplace or costly settlements and damage awards. Having a comprehensive bias-free policy as well as complaint and disciplinary procedures in place to prevent workplace harassment is critical. However, these alone will not prevent harassment in the workplace. It is only through training that employees and supervisors will learn to change their attitudes and behavior.

✓ Checklist

Training benefits

Training can achieve much of what the law requires that employers do to prevent and eliminate harassment, such as:

- ☐ Document that there is a policy against workplace harassment and that the policy was communicated.
- ☐ Underscore the employer's commitment.
- ☐ Make it easy for employees to know how to make complaints.
- ☐ Provide proof to any third party that an employee (including a manager or supervisor) was advised on a specific date, time and place about the organization's position on workplace harassment and about the various types of workplace harassment.

Legal reasons to train

There are several specific reasons from a legal perspective as to why HR should make sure that the workforce is trained about harassment and other inappropriate behavior. For more information about an employer's liability for workplace harassment, see Chapter 5.

◆ **Prevent liability for supervisor harassment.** Training can assist an employer's ability to prove both that it acted reasonably by teaching supervisors and employees workplace harassment prevention and by showing that the employee acted unreasonably because he or she was educated on harassment and the organization's complaint procedure, but failed to utilize it.

◆ **Prevent liability for coworker and non-employee harassment.** Employees must learn that they have a duty to report such harassment themselves, so that the employer is given the opportunity to promptly correct the situation and, therefore, avoid liability. Additionally, supervisors must be taught to recognize and address workplace harassment so that "known" harassment does not go uncorrected.

◆ **Prevent liability for punitive damages.** Documented training efforts can demonstrate an employer's strong commitment to a non-discriminatory work environment.

Best Practices
PPG Industries receives high marks from the EEOC

In looking at workplace rules, conditions and benefits, the EEOC in 1997 identified several companies that exhibited workplace practices characterized as "best." Making its list was PPG Industries, Inc., a manufacturer and distributor of glass products and specialty chemicals with headquarters in Pittsburgh, Pennsylvania.

PPG states that it is concerned about harassment, including sexual harassment. A comprehensive anti-harassment policy and follow-up training sessions were put in place in 1993 to ensure that employees are aware that sexual harassment (as well as racial, age, and other unlawful harassment) is prohibited.

Employees are informed that they may file an internal harassment complaint with any member of PPG management with whom they feel comfortable. PPG also communicates that that the complaint will be promptly and fairly investigated. In addition, the company provides guidance as to: (1) what sexual harassment is; (2) who is protected; (3) what preventive actions are to be taken; and (4) how complaints will be investigated.

Who to train

It used to be sufficient to train managers and supervisors about workplace harassment. However, that is no longer the case. Because it is clear that employers must take proactive measures to prevent and correct workplace harassment, HR must provide training to *both* supervisory personnel and employees.

Accommodations in training. HR has an obligation under the Americans with Disabilities Act to provide workers with disabilities with the opportunity to participate in training. Training opportunities cannot be denied because of the need to make reasonable accommodations to the training process, unless accommodation would be an undue hardship.

✓ ✓ **Checklist**

Accommodation suggestions

Accommodations that may be necessary, depending on the needs of particular workers, include:

- ☐ accessible locations and facilities for people with mobility disabilities;
- ☐ interpreters and note-takers for workers who have hearing impairments;
- ☐ materials in accessible formats;
- ☐ readers for people who have visual impairments, for people with learning disabilities, and for people with mental retardation;

> - [ ] captions for people who are hearing-impaired, and voice-overs for people who are visually impaired when audiovisual materials are used;
> - [ ] good general illumination for people with visual impairments and other disabilities, particularly good lighting on an interpreter;
> - [ ] clarification of concepts presented in training for people who have reading or other disabilities; and
> - [ ] individualized instruction for people with mental retardation and certain other disabilities.

When to train

To ensure that an employer's communication efforts are reasonable, training must occur regularly. What does this mean? It is best to train both employees and supervisors upon hire as a part of their orientation. Then, train periodically, such as annually.

If a complaint of harassment has been made or if harassment has been observed, it may be necessary to retrain the entire workforce or those members who may be lacking in the necessary understanding of appropriate behavior. If a complaint is found to have merit, this is a clear warning signal to HR that training efforts should be re-evaluated for effectiveness.

Training components

One of the primary goals of anti-harassment training is to effectively communicate the organization's clear policy against harassment and other types of inappropriate behavior in the workplace. Another equally important goal is to educate employees on how to recognize and confront harassment.

Training should include all forms of unlawful harassment, which consists of any conduct that shows hostility to another because of his or her race, religion, gender, national origin, age, disability, veteran status, or any other category protected by law. For more information on what constitutes harassment, see Chapters 2 and 3.

General training. The training program should teach both employees and supervisory personnel about:

◆ the organization's policy regarding workplace harassment;

◆ the complaint procedures to be followed for reporting harassment;

◆ the disciplinary measures that may be taken against persons who engage in harassment; and

◆ what is and is not harassing behavior.

Supervisory personnel. Because managers and supervisors are required to proactively respond to and report harassment, these individuals also need to learn:

◆ the seriousness of supervisor harassment;

◆ their duty to monitor the workplace and report harassment; and

◆ how to respond to a complaint of workplace harassment.

Communicating the policy

Employees and supervisory personnel need to be taught that the employer has in place a policy that strictly prohibits harassment and other forms of unlawful discrimination. Training should cover the key elements of the policy, particularly the complaint procedure. It should be emphasized that persons who report harassment will not be retaliated against for coming forward or for participating in an investigation.

It is also important to make clear that it is each person's responsibility to report suspected harassment by following the organization's complaint procedure. Employees need to understand that the organization must be made aware of inappropriate conduct in order to promptly investigate and take whatever action is necessary to retain a harassment-free work environment. You cannot overstate the organization's commitment. Let workers know that any complaints will be handled as confidentially as possible.

It is also a good idea to provide information about how suspected harassment will be investigated and what will happen to persons found to have engaged in inappropriate conduct. Again, be sure to stress that anyone involved in an investigation will be protected from retaliation.

DON'T
miss
this

Explaining harassment

Make it understandable

To be effective, training needs to make workplace harassment understandable. While the formal, legal definitions of workplace harassment should be presented, the training should also make workplace harassment easy to understand. This can be done by explaining in easy-to-understand terms what conduct the organization will and will not tolerate.

Provide real life examples. Examples of harassing conduct will be very informative. Give examples of some of the behaviors that could be considered harassment. If the policy prohibits inappropriate conduct, provide examples of such behavior as well.

DON'T miss this

It is best to train employees and supervisors to practice respect in the workplace, including inappropriate behavior that does not necessarily rise to the level of unlawful harassment but that could reasonably be offensive to another person. For example, if Vijay whistles at his coworker Gail every morning, this is probably not sexual harassment. But it is inappropriate conduct for the workplace. Gail could reasonably be offended by Vijay's behavior, and his conduct certainly does not serve any useful business purpose.

Also, the facts and myths surrounding sexual and other types of harassment should be discussed. For example, many individuals wrongly believe that only attractive, scantily clothed females are harassed. Or, some believe that people who are offended by ethnic jokes are over-sensitive or don't have a good sense of humor. Try to keep discussions as open and non-judgmental as possible.

A+ *Best Practices*

Training tools help reinforce learning

One way to gauge the trainees' understanding of the harassment concept is through the use of role-play. Use role-playing or a series of scenarios that focus on each type of behavior and the subtle differences in behavior. Role-playing can help provide employees with an understanding of what constitutes harassment, how to report incidents, how to state specific behavior and how to identify witnesses. An interactive discussion following the role-play activity is a good way to reinforce the concepts learned.

A self-assessment quiz can also be helpful. Use a quiz to examine the myths surrounding harassment, help employees recognize their own misconceptions and allow them to see what information they need for a complete understanding of what workplace harassment really is.

Explain the difference between verbal and physical harassment.

One way to increase understanding about harassing behavior is to compare the different types of behavior.

✓ *Checklist*

Harassment examples

Here are a few examples of verbal harassment:

☐ derogatory or vulgar comments regarding a person's protected characteristic (for example, race, national origin, age or gender);

☐ sexually suggestive or racially hostile language;

☐ remarks about a person's physical anatomy or characteristics; and

☐ distribution of written or graphic sexual or racially hostile materials.

> Physical harassment involves conduct like:
> ☐ touching another person in a sexually suggestive way;
> ☐ touching another person so as to invade their personal privacy;
> ☐ pushing or shoving another person; and
> ☐ obscene gestures.

Sexual harassment examples. Because sexual harassment raises complex issues, it is a good idea to have a separate discussion about what behavior may be sexually harassing. Provide examples of both coworker harassment and supervisor harassment.

Labor attorney Edward Cherof, a partner with the Atlanta office of the Jackson Lewis law firm, provides these examples of conduct which have either singly or in combination been found to create or contribute to sexually hostile environment:

◆ Obscene or "dirty" remarks
◆ Obscene or "dirty" jokes
◆ Sexual gestures
◆ Pornographic materials
◆ Nude or semi-nude photographs
◆ Touching
◆ Talking about the sexual activities or desires of the alleged harasser, harassment victim or other person
◆ Sexual advances
◆ Sexual graffiti in rest rooms
◆ Obscene cartoons
◆ Acts of physical aggression
◆ Intimidation
◆ Acts of hostility
◆ Presence of "exotic" dancers at parties
◆ Vendor's calendars featuring semi-nude persons in sexually suggestive or submissive poses
◆ Unequal treatment based on sex

Best Practices

Training focuses on creating a respectful workplace

One company's training program on sexual harassment and other inappropriate conduct attempts to create an atmosphere of respect for fellow workers. The training is a half-day interactive workshop facilitated by a trained team of one male and one female employee. The groups are comprised of about 25 to 30 employees and are mixed according to the blend of males and females in the particular work group.

Rather than focusing on how to stay out of legal trouble, the program builds positive workplace relationships. Both managers as well as employees are trained. The company wants all personnel to understand that they all play a role in creating an environment of mutual respect free from discrimination and harassment

The program begins with a video depicting two company bowling teams that are talking about a fellow employee named Rachel, who has just accused her supervisor of sexual harassment. The video depicts employees' comments like:

◆ "She's ruined his career"
◆ "She was just a flirt"
◆ "She was really being harassed"
◆ "He should be fired"

The facilitators break the employees into small groups and then ask employees to describe what they saw in the video and to think about the issues that arise as a result of sexual harassment. Participants then are asked to develop definitions of sexual discrimination and sexual harassment. The company's definition of sexual harassment is explained, along with the definitions of sexual discrimination and harassment in the EEOC's Guidelines. The video is followed by a two-minute taped interview with the company CEO. The rest of the program is based on seven more vignettes, followed by a discussion led by facilitators.

Manager and supervisor training

The law is clear that employers will be liable for the actions of their managers and supervisors. Organizations are basically self-insuring against improper acts by these supervisory personnel. Employers should regularly train managers and supervisors to understand what workplace harassment is, as well as their responsibility to refrain from harassment and prevent it from taking place.

In addition, supervisor training should explain management's responsibility for enforcing the bias-free policy and the steps that managers and supervisors should follow when they suspect workplace harassment is taking place. Supervisory personnel need to specifically understand their responsibilities to recognize workplace harassment and to immediately report it to HR and other appropriate officials.

WHAT you need to know

An organization's managers and supervisors play an important role in the communication and enforcement of the bias-free policy. They are often the first to hear a complaint of harassment or to see inappropriate activity in the workplace.

Don't just stop with training. HR must ensure that training is effective by evaluating supervisor performance in the area of maintaining a harassment-free workplace.

Avoiding supervisory harassment

Managers and supervisors should learn why it is so important that they understand what workplace harassment is. HR needs to make sure that persons with supervisory authority understand the seriousness of harassment. This includes teaching them that the organization will be automatically liable for harassment committed by those with supervisory authority and that it may also be liable for any harassment that supervisors know about but fail to report to HR.

Training should inform managers and supervisors that because of their status in the company, their actions will be judged more severely. And, because of the problems posed by supervisor-subordinate romances, these folks should be taught their responsibilities with regard to such relationships. If your organization has a policy against office romances, go over the policy during supervisor training.

It is also a good idea that training inform managers and supervisors that they can be personally liable for some forms of harassment under state laws and that the employer may seek damages from supervisory personnel if their actions result in liability against the organization.

Monitoring the workplace

Like employees, managers and supervisors must be taught what behavior is considered workplace harassment. Not only does HR want to prevent supervisory personnel from engaging in any potentially harassing conduct, but they also need managers and supervisors to be able to recognize harassment in the workplace. They must be taught that they are responsible not only for their own behavior, but for the conduct of those in their work groups. This means not only identifying inappropriate conduct in the workplace, but also immediately alerting HR to it.

Many managers and supervisors may hesitate to get involved in a potentially harassing situation between coworkers because they believe it to be too personal. For example, if Sam knows that his two subordinates, Arnez and Maria, are romantically involved, he may feel that he has no business getting involved in their relationship or their rumored break up. But harassment can occur between romantically involved coworkers and Sam needs to be on the look out for potential issues. Training needs to emphasize that workplace harassment is always a workplace issue—not a personal issue.

Responding to a complaint

All supervisory personnel need to become familiar with the organization's internal complaint procedure for handling harassment complaints. Training should make clear who managers and supervisors need to contact when an individual comes to them with a complaint. Make sure they know their responsibility to report a complaint even if the complaining employee asks that the manager or supervisor keep it secret.

Demonstrate how to respond. Because reports of harassment are often first presented to managers and supervisors, it is crucial to train these folks about how to respond to a complaint. Teach them to act as a LEADER: Listen, Encourage, Ask questions, Document, Explain and Respond. (For more details, see Chapter 9).

Have managers and supervisors engage in role-play of a discussion with an alleged victim. Discuss what worked and what didn't go so well. By practicing how to best respond and discussing mistakes, supervisory personnel will be better prepared and will be more comfortable should the situation arise.

Explain the investigation process. Even if a manager or supervisor will not be chosen to conduct an investigation, it is important for him or her to understand the process. The manager or supervisor may be called upon to assist in the investigation and may even be interviewed about his or her knowledge of the facts. By understanding the investigatory procedure, the manager or supervisor can provide greater assistance, ultimately helping to protect the employer from liability.

WHAT you need to know

Workers often question their manager or supervisor about the investigation process once word gets out that a workplace harassment complaint has been made. In such instances, the manager or supervisor must be able to appropriately answer employee questions in order to quash any rumors and alleviate any fears of retaliation.

Stress confidentiality. The need for confidentiality should be emphasized, and supervisory personnel should be instructed regarding how to communicate with witnesses and other members of their departments to maintain confidentiality. Because retaliation against an employer who brings a complaint is illegal, managers and supervisors must be taught to ensure employees are not being retaliated against.

Documenting training efforts

Organizations that train their employees and supervisory personnel on workplace harassment and other EEO practices must carefully document such efforts. Employees often say that they do not use a complaint procedure because they were not aware one existed or they thought it would do no good to complain. Training can help show that these excuses for failure to use a complaint procedure are unreasonable.

Therefore, HR must keep track of who has completed training. Keep good track of the dates and times of training sessions and attendance. Also document the contents of the training in order to demonstrate what was actually covered during the training. Regularly review the documentation to make sure that everyone has been trained who needs to be.

Legal experts recommend having employees sign a document acknowledging that they have completed anti-harassment training and understood it.

Evaluation

The program evaluation should assess whether or not the training enhanced employees' knowledge and understanding of workplace harassment, reaffirmed the organization's policy on workplace harassment, led to employee behavior change, and ultimately improved morale and productivity. Follow-up approaches could include surveys or small group discussions or interviews with participants. Long-term follow up might be measured by reviewing performance appraisals and grievance and complaint rates.

Truly reliable testing and measuring to determine training effectiveness often requires the expertise of educators, psychologists and statisticians to design and implement measurement methods that meet standards of validity and reliability. However, even without a formal validation method, measuring results can provide a good indication of whether a training program has worked.

Did they learn what they needed to? To determine whether harassment training has been effective, employee surveys should assess the following:

- ◆ Whether or not the employee understands what behaviors constitute workplace harassment.
- ◆ Whether or not the employee understands the employer's attitude toward workplace harassment.
- ◆ Whether or not the employee knows the employer's procedure for filing a complaint of workplace harassment.
- ◆ Whether or not the employee understands the disciplinary sanctions for workplace harassment.

Did they like the training? In addition to gauging the success of training to measure what has actually been learned, HR may want to ask trainees how they felt about the training and what they think they've gained from it.

Participant reaction, of course, won't all be positive. Some trainees will tell HR that they found the training to be a waste of time. Their reactions may be based on many things other than what they did or did not learn. But if you do get a large number of negative reactions, you have a clear signal that there is something wrong with your program, your instructor or both. Ask participants specific questions, such as:

- ◆ What did you learn?
- ◆ What were the most/least helpful parts of the course?
- ◆ How could the instructor have been more effective?
- ◆ What recommendations/changes should be made in this program?
- ◆ Was enough time dedicated to each subject?
- ◆ How will you apply what you learned in this course when you return to your job?

The Quiz

1. Who should be trained on workplace harassment prevention?
   a. Employees.
   b. Supervisors.
   c. Both choices a and b.
   d. Neither choice a or b.

2. It is important that employers who provide anti-harassment training carefully document such efforts.　　❑ True　　❑ False

3. Which of the following is not a true statement about harassment prevention training? (Select one).
   a. Effective training helps prevent liability for supervisor, coworker and non-employee harassment.
   b. Training is only necessary if a complaint of harassment has been made against a supervisor.
   c. Training should include real life examples of potentially harassing conduct.
   d. Supervisors should learn what to do if an employee comes to them with a complaint of harassment.

4. It is not a good idea to have an employee sign a document acknowledging that they have completed training and understood it.　　❑ True　　❑ False

Answer key: 1.c, 2.T, 3.b, 4.F.

Managers and supervisors: special concerns and challenges

Liability for harassment by supervisors.................................... 116

    Supervisors who engage in harassment 116

    BEST PRACTICES: Handle supervisor
        harassment claims with care.. 117

    Supervisors who fail to report harassment.......................... 118

Supervisory responsibilities 118

    Act as a role model 119

    Take appropriate action... 120

    Foster respect 121

    Anti-harassment guidelines 122

Monitoring managers and supervisors...................................... 124

The Quiz... 126

You receive word from your in-house counsel that an EEOC complaint has been lodged against your organization. A customer service representative, Miriam, is claiming to be a victim of age and disability harassment. She further claims that the organization knew about the harassment and failed to take corrective action. You have no record of an internal harassment complaint being filed by Miriam. You question her supervisor, Ling, about the situation. He admits that Miriam did complain that her coworkers were harassing her. However, he states that Miriam only brought up this "supposed harassment" after being issued a final warning for tardiness and poor performance. Convinced that Miriam was "making things up in hopes of saving her job," Ling says that he dismissed the complaint as a sham. Did Ling handle the situation appropriately? If Miriam was in fact a harassment victim, did she provide the organization with sufficient notice by complaining to a supervisor? Besides assisting legal counsel with investigating and responding to Miriam's complaint, what steps should HR take to make sure its supervisory employees know how to properly respond to future complaints of harassment?

Liability for harassment by supervisors

The law has made clear that both human resources and supervisory staff share the task of preventing and eliminating harassment in the workplace, and ultimately protecting an organization from liability. Why does supervisory staff share such a critical task? Managers and supervisors are responsible not only for their behaviors, but the conduct of all those in their work groups. To prevent potential liability, supervisory personnel must not only avoid engaging in any inappropriate actions that may be considered harassing, they must also identify inappropriate conduct in the workplace and take action to promptly alert HR.

WHAT you need to know

Management attorney William C. Martucci suggests that a harassing supervisor is like a defective product. If a company produces a product and sends it out into commerce, and the product later explodes due to no fault of the consumer, the company will be required to pay for all damages caused by the explosion. In human terms, if a company puts a manager into the workplace who initiates, participates in or condones unlawful harassment (in effect, "explodes") then the company will similarly be automatically liable for the harm the "defective" supervisor causes.

Supervisors who engage in harassment

If a manager or supervisor engages in workplace harassment, the employer may be automatically liable if the victim decides to sue the organization. If a lawsuit is brought, it will not matter whether HR knew about the conduct, or even if it should have known about it. If the victim of the harassment suffered an employment action (for example, was fired, demoted or reassigned), the organization will have no defense to the charge.

Even if the victim does not suffer an employment action (for example, the supervisor doesn't fire or demote the victim, but constantly makes racist and offensive comments), the organization will still be automatically liable unless it can prove both:

1. that it took reasonable precautions to prevent the harassment; and
2. that the victim failed to take reasonable action to prevent the harm.

For more details on employer liability for manager or supervisor harassment, see Chapter 5.

Best Practices

Handle supervisor harassment claims with care

HR must quickly address a complaint of supervisory harassment by investigating the charges and taking appropriate action as necessary. But HR must also take special care not to overreact if a harassment claim is brought against a supervisor, warns management attorney William C. Martucci.

Because this is a delicate and challenging area, HR professionals must work with management to maintain the delicate balance between the rights of their employees to be free from workplace harassment, and the rights of supervisors to be free from invasion of privacy and defamation. A panic-stricken employer that fails to fully investigate a harassment complaint and instead immediately fires the supervisor may face an entirely different legal challenge—the alleged harasser's claim of unfair treatment.

Supervisors who fail to report harassment

An organization will be liable for workplace harassment committed by a victim's coworker if the organization was aware or should have been aware of the harassment, and failed to stop it. An employer "is aware" of harassment if the behavior is reported to, or observed by, a manager or supervisor.

This is because a manager or supervisor has the authority to stop the harassment or, at the very least, to bring the harassment to the attention of someone who can stop it. Accordingly, if a manager or supervisor knows about harassment and fails to take steps to stop it, the employer faces legal trouble.

> **Example:** *Shaw, a supervisor, notices members of his team ridiculing one of their coworkers about her physical disability. Shaw perceives the joking as innocent banter and chooses not to do anything about it. If the behavior is so pervasive as to create a hostile environment, and Shaw fails to alert HR so that an investigation can begin, his employer may be deemed to be "aware" of the conduct and wind up in court defending a harassment lawsuit.*

Think back to Ling, who failed to alert HR to Miriam's complaint of harassment. Ling took it upon himself to decide that Miriam's complaint was baseless. This was a very bad judgment call on Ling's part. If Miriam is in fact a victim of unlawful harassment, the organization may be liable based on Ling's notice of the behavior. And even if it turns out that Miriam's complaint does not have merit, it would have been much better for all concerned if HR had been given the opportunity to resolve the situation before Miriam decided to go to the EEOC.

Supervisory responsibilities

Supervisory employees play a critical role in preventing and eliminating unlawful harassment and discrimination. How can managers and supervisors assist HR in carrying out the organization's anti-harassment efforts? By doing the following:

- acting as a role model for the rest of the organization;
- taking appropriate action in response to inappropriate behavior; and
- fostering respect in the workplace.

Act as a role model

Managers and supervisors must serve as role models for the rest of the organization. Their actions must send a clear message to employees that workplace harassment and discrimination will not be tolerated under any circumstances. They must not engage in behavior that could arguably be perceived as offensive.

This includes making sure that what they say cannot be misconstrued as harassment. Inappropriate statements made by supervisors or managers often become key parts of an EEOC or court case involving an employee's claim of harassment or other discrimination.

Worst case scenario

Improper statements by supervisors

Here are some examples of statements made by supervisors that wound up being used as evidence against their respective employers:

- A supervisor's reference to female employees as "girls" and to male employees as "men" was evidence of race and sex discrimination. The term "girl" could refer to a repulsive historical image in the minds of African American employees and also implied to white females historical attitudes of female inferiority.
- A supervisor's religious preaching showed that an employer failed to provide a workplace free of religious intimidation. Employees could believe that job security would be affected by their reaction to the supervisor's religious statements.
- A manager's statement at a business dinner to a female coworker that he had heard that she had been seen engaging in sexual activity with another female constituted sexual harassment.

- ◆ Remarks by supervisors referring to a Chinese worker as a "chink" and as "tight eye" were the main pieces of evidence used to find that a racially hostile work environment existed that unlawfully forced the worker to resign.
- ◆ A manager's use of the phrase "old dogs don't know how to hunt" could suggest age discrimination against a 63-year-old employee.
- ◆ Performance evaluation statements that described a female accountant as "macho," advised her to "take a course in charm school," and suggested that she "overcompensated for being a woman," was evidence of unlawful sexual stereotyping.

Supervisors speak for the organization. The key lesson for HR to take away from the above examples is that statements made by managers and supervisors can be directly attributed to their employer. Supervisory members are considered to be *agents* of the organization. Any statements made by a manager or supervisor can be attributed to the employer and used as evidence to show that an employer acted improperly.

So what can HR do? Instruct supervisors and managers to be careful to make statements that are only related to their job of managing people to meet organizational goals.

Example: Maya is a supervisor who subjects a 68-year-old employee to abusive language and abusive discipline. If Maya subjects all employees—young and old—to the same abusive behavior, she has not engaged in illegal age harassment. Nevertheless, Maya's behavior is inappropriate. It demonstrates poor leadership qualities and reflects negatively on both Maya and the organization.

Take appropriate action

Managers and supervisors must also be prepared to respond to unlawful behavior. When confronted with a harassment complaint or when they see behavior that is inappropriate, supervisory staff must be able to swiftly address the complaint or stop the conduct. They must take all allegations seriously and never dismiss a complaint as trivial.

This does not mean that managers and supervisors must take on the entire responsibility for handling harassment and discrimination. They must work together with HR and other representatives charged with the responsibility to monitor the workplace.

> *To make sure that supervisory staff are prepared to handle a complaint of workplace harassment, teach them to act as a "LEADER": Listen, Encourage, Ask Questions, Document, Explain and Respond. See Chapter 9 for more details.*

DON'T
miss
this

Consider the situation with Ling. He failed to responsibly exercise his supervisory duties when he chose to dismiss Miriam's harassment claim as a sham. Instead of acting on his own, Ling should have sought out HR's assistance in handling the situation.

Foster respect

Managers and supervisors must also set higher standards of conduct by requiring respect in the workplace. They can enforce higher standards by prohibiting all types of conduct that may be offensive to employees.

Not all conduct that is offensive or even vulgar violates the law. But managers and supervisors should not be allowed to tolerate offensive conduct because they think it is not illegal. Any time offensive conduct is allowed by a manager or supervisor, an employer risks not only a harassment lawsuit, but also decreased morale and high turnover.

> **Example:** *Ruth overhears one her direct reports, Vincent, tell a group of female coworkers that they should wear skirts more often to "pretty up the office." Although this statement by itself is probably not sexual harassment, it is inappropriate. Ruth should counsel Vincent about proper behavior in the workplace. It would also be a good idea to alert HR that harassment prevention training may be in order.*

Anti-harassment guidelines

HR can prepare managers and supervisors to help lead the organization's efforts to prevent and eliminate harassment in the workplace by requiring them to follow these anti-harassment guidelines:

1. Understand what workplace harassment is. A manager or supervisor will not be able to prevent workplace harassment without first knowing what it is. In order to recognize and eliminate harassment in the workplace, supervisory personnel must actively learn what workplace harassment is and how it can occur.

2. Refrain from inappropriate behavior. Managers and supervisors must serve as role models for appropriate behavior in the workplace. They must act professionally at all times and under all circumstances. Moreover, they must *not* guess that otherwise inappropriate conduct is okay because it does not offend a particular audience.

3. Communicate the bias-free policy. Managers and supervisors must feel comfortable raising the issue of harassment and inappropriate conduct with employees. They must express strong disapproval of inappropriate conduct and tell employees what to do if they are confronted with offensive behavior. They must be prepared to explain the disciplinary sanctions that will be applied to harassers. And they must regularly and clearly communicate the organization's bias-free policy to employees.

4. Monitor the work environment. Managers and supervisors should never assume that everything is okay because nobody has complained. They must tell any employee who is observed engaging in inappropriate or unprofessional conduct to stop it and document that the employee was told to stop. If the conduct continues they must follow the organization's disciplinary procedure accordingly.

5. Respond appropriately to complaints. Managers and supervisors must follow and enforce the organization's internal complaint procedure that encourages employees to come forward with allegations of workplace harassment. They must make all complaints as confidential as possible, but never agree to keep a complaint secret.

They must reassure employees that no retaliation will be taken against someone who comes forward with a complaint.

6. Report potential harassment to HR. Managers and supervisors must never attempt to resolve a harassment problem alone. They must immediately report any concerns or complaints to HR and/or to any other company representatives designated to handle harassment and other EEO concerns.

7. Take every complaint seriously. One common trap for supervisory personnel is the complaint that "doesn't appear very important." But all workplace harassment complaints must be taken seriously. Managers and supervisors must work together with HR to investigate every complaint promptly and thoroughly.

8. Act immediately to stop harassment. Managers and supervisors must never delay necessary efforts to eliminate harassment. They must work with HR to take action as soon as harassment is alleged or observed. This includes following up to make sure that the harassment does not continue.

9. Ensure that retaliation does not occur. Managers and supervisors must take immediate action to stop any retaliation against a harassment victim or witness. If an employee complains of harassment by an individual with higher authority, supervisory personnel must work with HR to take measures that ensure the alleged harasser is not in a position to affect the complaining employee's job status.

10. Don't let an employee walk away frustrated. If a report of harassment cannot be resolved to the complaining employee's satisfaction, it is important that the employee's manager or supervisor work with HR to make sure that the employee does not walk away frustrated and angry because "no one cares" or "no one really understood." He or she should make sure the employee feels secure about the immediate future. Because the employee may fear further harassment or retaliation, the supervisor should explain the steps that the employee should take to report any such incidents.

Monitoring managers and supervisors

As part of the anti-harassment program, HR should regularly monitor supervisory employees for compliance with the organization's anti-harassment and EEO policies. HR should also see to it that such compliance is included in formal evaluations. The monitoring function will be particularly important for employers that have supervisors at distant locations without upper management on-site.

WHAT you need to know

HR should make the elimination of harassment in the workplace one of the essential functions of managers' and supervisors' jobs. This includes making it their responsibility to cooperate with the organization and its monitoring efforts by providing honest feedback concerning their peers and managers when requested to do so. Conversely, they should welcome constructive criticism from others, and never retaliate against peers or subordinates who provide honest feedback concerning their behavior.

One way to regularly monitor supervisory staff for anti-harassment behavior is to include EEO preventive practices as part of all managers' and supervisors' job responsibilities. To make sure they are carrying out this function, feedback should be requested in the same way as it is with any other supervisory responsibilities. And if a manager or supervisor fails to report harassing, discriminatory or inappropriate conduct, appropriate disciplinary action should be taken.

✓✓ *Checklist*

Anti-harassment management of supervisory staff

Follow these steps to help prevent legal problems and foster a happier work environment.

☐ Screen applicants for supervisory jobs to see if they have a record of engaging in harassment.

☐ Conduct periodic training to ensure that managers and supervisors understand their responsibilities under the anti-harassment policy.

☐ Educate supervisory staff to enforce the policy and to be sensitive to improper conduct. Teach them to take appropriate actions and remedies.

☐ Require supervisory personnel to immediately report suspected harassment to HR.

☐ Instruct all managers and supervisors, whether they are designated to take complaints or not, to address or report all complaints of harassment, even if the complaint does not conform to the complaint procedures.

☐ Include EEO preventive practices as part of a supervisor's job responsibilities.

☐ Keep track of supervisors' conduct to make sure that they are carrying out their responsibilities.

☐ Periodically request feedback from peers and/or subordinates concerning supervisors' and managers' performance in terms of EEO practices, harassment behavior, professionalism and attitude.

☐ Keep all records of complaints and review for possible patterns of harassment by the same individual.

The Quiz

1. If an employee complains to her manager about age harassment, the manager should *not*:
   a. Immediately report the concern to HR.
   b. Attempt to resolve the harassment problem alone.
   c. Take the complaint seriously if it doesn't seem very important.
   d. Refer to the organization's complaint procedure.

2. Managers and supervisors must work together with HR to take action as soon as harassment is reported or observed.   ☐ True   ☐ False

3. Which of the following are ways that HR may monitor its supervisory staff for anti-harassment behavior?
   a. Include EEO preventive practices as part of the supervisors' job responsibilities.
   b. Periodically request feedback from peers concerning supervisors' performance in terms of EEO practices, harassing behavior, professionalism and attitude.
   c. Both choices a and b.
   d. None of the above.

4. Monitoring supervisory staff for compliance with the employer's anti-harassment and EEO policies is less important for employers that have supervisors at distant locations without upper management on-site.   ☐ True   ☐ False

Answer key: 1.b, 2.T, 3.c, 4.F

Investigating harassment

Becoming aware of harassment 128

The initial complaint 129

    Act as a "LEADER" 129

    The reluctant employee 132

    The delayed complaint... 133

    BEST PRACTICES: What to tell someone
        who reports harassment 133

Starting the investigation 134

    BEST PRACTICES: Prompt investigation
        helps school district avoid liability 135

    What are the steps? 135

    Who should investigate?... 136

Obtaining relevant information... 137

Conducting the interviews 138

    The complainant 138

    The accused.. 141

    Other witnesses 143

    Determining credibility 145

Documenting the process.. 146

Maintaining confidentiality... 146

    Understanding and avoiding defamation.............................. 147

Protecting the accuser and the accused 149

The Quiz.. 150

Dimitri enters the HR office early one morning and asks if he can speak to someone in private. You usher him into your office and ask him to take a seat. Dimitri seems very nervous and keeps fiddling with his hands. Before you have a chance to ask him why he's there, Dimitri blurts out that he is having problems with several of his coworkers and doesn't know what to do. He says, "I may not be as manly as the rest of the crew, but I am not who they think I am. They think I like men but I'm not like that. I'm tired of all the pranks. Look at this. They think it's funny but I don't." Dimitri shows you a cartoon that shows two men in a sexually explicit pose. Someone has handwritten the word "Dimitri" on the cartoon, along with an arrow pointing to one of the men. You ask Dimitri where he found the cartoon and he says, "You know what. Never mind. This was a mistake, I think I should go." What should you do? What if Dimitri doesn't want to provide further details? Even if he does, what steps should you take based on his story?

Becoming aware of harassment

HR may become aware of potential workplace harassment in many ways. Some of the more common include:

◆ An anonymous complaint.

◆ A complaint by another employee or someone outside of the organization.

◆ A complaint by the harassed employee to a member of management—typically their manager or supervisor—or to another person in a position to do something about it, such as a security guard or nurse.

◆ A complaint by the harassed employee to human resources.

◆ Observance of the harassment by management or by a member of HR.

WHAT you need to know

Another way that HR may become aware of workplace harassment is by the receipt of a formal complaint from the EEOC or other administrative agency. Because of the various legal implications created by the government's involvement, special investigatory precautions may be necessary. Therefore, it is best for HR to immediately consult legal counsel for guidance once a formal charge of harassment has been received.

Regardless of how HR finds out about it, one of the biggest mistakes HR can make is to ignore or improperly respond to harassment in the workplace. It is unlikely that HR is intentionally ignoring harassment. Rather, a worker may be embarrassed or scared about inappropriate behavior and therefore not come right out and clearly say what has occurred. Meanwhile HR professionals, concerned about employee privacy rights, are cautious about making additional inquiries. Therefore, it is crucial that HR create an atmosphere where employees feel comfortable raising issues concerning harassing or otherwise discriminatory workplace behavior.

> **Example:** *Suppose Elliott makes repeated negative comments to his coworker, Yelena, about her psychological disability. Yelena may feel uncomfortable talking to HR about the nature of Elliott's comments and instead complain that Elliott "treats her funny" and is "mean" to her. If HR dismisses Yelena's complaint as insignificant and tells her not to worry so much about how others treat her, she probably will not feel comfortable raising the issue again. But if Elliott's behavior is considered unlawful harassment, the employer could be in legal trouble because Yelena complained about the behavior and the employer failed to investigate and take prompt, corrective action.*

The initial complaint

Act as a "LEADER"

Often, HR becomes aware of potential harassment because an employee brings a complaint to HR or to a member of management. Because this will often be the first time harassment is made known, it is vital that the person who receives a complaint of harassment—whether the HR professional, a manager or a supervisor—be prepared to respond properly by acting as a "LEADER":

Listen

Encourage

Ask questions

Document

Explain

Respond

Listen. To effectively address a harassment complaint, the person taking the complaint must be a good listener, able to create an atmosphere where employees feel comfortable raising sensitive issues. Every complaint of harassment must be taken seriously, no matter how silly or insignificant the behavior may seem at first to be. Don't assume someone is being too sensitive. Try to use the employee's perspective.

DON'T miss this

Part of being a good listener may require reading between the lines. For example, sexual harassment is not an easy topic for any employee to bring up. The employee may be embarrassed, afraid of losing his or her job, or just a bad communicator. Listen for code words when someone complains about another's behavior. For instance, does he or she "feel uncomfortable" or "uneasy?" Is he or she being asked not to have to work with a particular person because they "don't get along?" Does a coworker "treat her funny" or "act creepy around him?"

Encourage. Try to make the employee feel comfortable while maintaining a professional attitude. Acknowledge that bringing a harassment complaint is a difficult thing to do and that it is normal for the employee to feel uneasy. Reassure him or her that the information will be kept as confidential as possible, but not secret.

Ask questions. Get answers. Who did what to whom, when, where, how and why? Find out what the employee would like to see happen as a result of the complaint.

Document. Immediately create a written record of the employee's statements. Do not wait to document. It is important that records of a harassment complaint reflect exactly what was said. Ask the person complaining to review and sign your documentation to reflect that it is accurate. If the employee is unwilling to provide a written statement, take note of that fact and continue with the interview anyway.

Explain. Explain the workplace harassment policy to the employee. Provide assurances that no retaliation or negative employment action will be taken against the employee for making the complaint. Answer any questions that he or she may have.

Respond. Immediately report the conversation as outlined in your organization's harassment policy. If you are charged with the authority to initiate an investigation into the matter, take the necessary steps to do so.

Worst case scenario

A company that didn't know about harassment and therefore failed to investigate it was still responsible legally because two supervisors were aware of the situation. The victim, Sharon, worked as an operator at a chemical plant. She was the only female on her shift. After Sharon was asked to give a talk to a group of girls that would be touring the plant on "Take Your Daughter To Work Day," several of her coworkers stopped talking to her. One coworker told others not to follow Sharon's instructions without confirming with him first. Coworkers also made offensive remarks and played practical jokes on Sharon that made her seem incompetent and jeopardized her safety. One incident involved someone placing in her locker a Bible verse that read, "[a] women should learn in quietness and full submission. I do not permit a woman to teach or have authority over a man, she must be silent."

The company lost the lawsuit that was filed against it because it failed to make a good faith effort to stop the behavior. Sharon complained about the harassment to her supervisor, who also witnessed the harassment. She also complained during sessions of a company-sponsored support group that were attended by her supervisor's boss. Yet neither the supervisor nor his boss investigated Sharon's allegations and both failed to discipline the coworker whose behavior toward her was well known. The only investigation occurred after Sharon found the Bible verse. At this point coworkers were interviewed using a list of yes-or-no questions. The investigation was dropped when the coworkers denied knowledge of the incident.

Solution. HR must ensure that managers always follow the "R" (respond) in LEADER to ensure that if a complaint of workplace of harassment is made, it is investigated. Once HR knows about harassment, it must initiate a thorough investigation and take corrective action as necessary.

The reluctant employee

What if an employee complains about harassment but asks that his or her complaint be kept secret? Even if a person who reports workplace harassment asks that no action be taken, an employer that does nothing in response can be held liable for the harassment. HR has been made aware of the situation and must now investigate and take any necessary corrective action.

HR should therefore explain to the employee that the employer has a strict policy forbidding harassment and discrimination in the workplace and has a legal duty to investigate the problem now that it has been raised. Assure the employee that the matter will be handled as discreetly as possible and that no negative employment action will result from the employee's complaint. Then investigate the harassment complaint.

WHAT you need to know

An investigation is obviously hindered if the employee refuses to give any further information about the conduct. This makes it especially important for HR to document the employee's failure to cooperate, document any answers to questions the employee may have provided, and document any further investigatory actions that are taken by the organization. HR should also encourage the employee to come forward again if the harassment continues and follow up with the employee.

Think back to Dimitri. He came to you complaining of harassment but became reluctant during your conversation. This is obviously a sensitive issue for Dimitri and, as such, it was probably very difficult for him to come to you in the first place. It is important to reassure Dimitri that HR will handle the situation as discreetly as possible and protect him from retaliation. At the same time, Dimitri must understand that HR will be investigating the matter so that necessary steps can be taken to end any inappropriate behavior in the workplace.

The delayed complaint

What if an employee reports harassment that supposedly occurred several years ago? Take the complaint seriously and investigate as you would a current claim. It is possible that the employee cannot go to a government agency or sue in court because too much time has passed under EEOC or other legal rules for filing charges or suing in court. However, HR can never be too sure. Therefore, in addition to the basic information you would ask of the employee, also ask if any similar activity has occurred recently. Ask whether some form of retaliation occurred because of the incident.

Then investigate to see if other workers have similar complaints. Experts on harassment warn that in many cases there will be a pattern of harassing behavior by a supervisor that is repeated over the years with different employees. Remember that there is no "time limit" on your corporate policy. Regardless of your legal liability, as an HR professional, you know that sexual or any other type of harassment can poison a working environment, resulting in increased turnover and lost productivity at the very least. So the passage of time is no reason to dismiss the importance of a complaint.

Best Practices

What to tell someone who reports harassment

Lisa Lavelle Burke and Doug Mishkin, attorneys at Patton Boggs, LLP, provided this "to do" list for the initial meeting with an employee who has brought a complaint.

◆ Thank the person raising the issue for doing so.
◆ Inform the person raising the issue that the organization does not permit any retaliation or reprisal for bringing a legitimate issue to light, and advise the employee that if he or she believes retaliation is occurring, to report it immediately.

◆ Tell the employee that if an investigation is needed, he or she will be notified and will be told who will conduct the investigation.

◆ Tell the employee that you will limit the disclosure to those people having a legitimate reason to know, and instruct the employee to do the same. Inform the employee that he or she, as well as all individuals involved in an investigation, have a duty to keep investigative information confidential.

◆ Let the employee know that the person conducting the investigation will be getting back to him or her from time to time during the investigation and that his or her continued cooperation in the investigation will be necessary to reach a resolution.

◆ Ask the employee for suggestions on how the matter could best be resolved. Does the employee have any suggestions? The employee's answer will be helpful to determining how to proceed.

◆ Let the employee know that while the employer will make a final decision regarding the best way to resolve the issue, the employee's input is valuable and will be considered seriously.

◆ Thank the employee again for raising the issue and express the organization's commitment to resolving the matter in a timely manner.

Starting the investigation

Once inappropriate conduct is reported and HR knows about the problem, it is necessary to conduct an immediate internal investigation. The best policy is to investigate all complaints and appearances of workplace harassment and to make a determination based purely on the facts. The quicker the response to a workplace harassment complaint, the lower the risk of liability. Also, unnecessarily delaying or even extending the investigation traumatizes an organization and makes witness testimony increasingly unreliable.

Best Practices

Prompt investigation helps school district avoid liability

A school district was able to avoid liability on a teacher's sexual harassment claim for two reasons: first, the teacher failed to make known a principal's inappropriate actions and second, the district promptly investigated the principal's behavior as soon as it became aware of the problem.

The teacher claimed in court that the principal snapped her bra, insinuated that she was a lesbian and made crude comments. She was interviewed when the district was investigating anonymous harassment complaints that were made concerning the principal. But the teacher did not report the principal's conduct toward her. Although the investigation failed to uncover evidence of harassment, the principal was warned about his behavior. It was only after the harassment continued that the teacher filed a formal complaint. In response, the district promptly conducted another investigation and ultimately reassigned the principal to another position.

What are the steps?

The goal of a workplace harassment investigation is to gather all of the facts so that HR can determine whether inappropriate conduct did or did not occur. These are the steps to follow:

- ◆ Obtain relevant information.
- ◆ Conduct the interviews.
- ◆ Document the investigation.
- ◆ Maintain confidentiality.
- ◆ Protect the accused and the accuser.

According to a 1999 survey by the Society for Human Resource Management (SHRM), 86 percent of responding companies had established formal processes to investigate complaints of workplace harassment.

DON'T
miss
this

Who should investigate?

In many cases, HR will be responsible for the investigation. Be sure that HR professionals are thoroughly trained before being assigned investigative duties. Such training should include learning the skills that are required for interviewing witnesses and evaluating credibility. Does your HR department have a clear understanding of what constitutes workplace harassment? In particular, if he or she has not already done so, the person who will be conducting the investigation should become familiar with the definition of workplace harassment and examples of behaviors that have been found to be harassment. Reading this booklet is a good start.

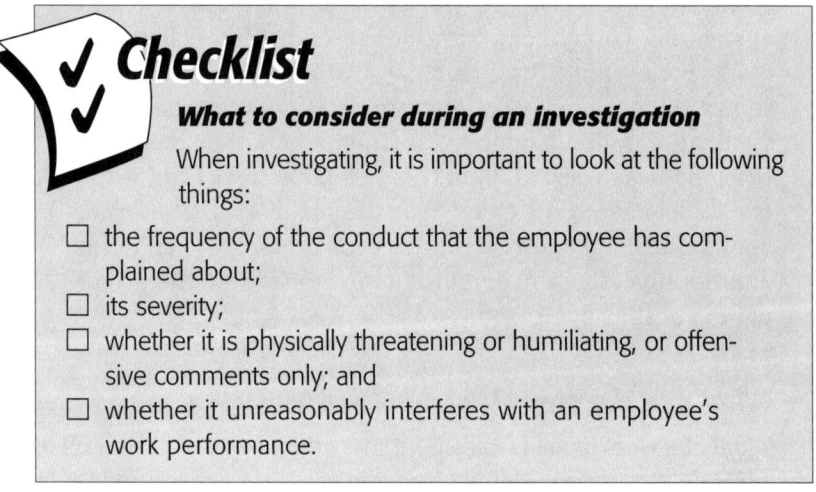

✔ *Checklist*
✔

What to consider during an investigation

When investigating, it is important to look at the following things:

- ☐ the frequency of the conduct that the employee has complained about;
- ☐ its severity;
- ☐ whether it is physically threatening or humiliating, or offensive comments only; and
- ☐ whether it unreasonably interferes with an employee's work performance.

In some organizations, HR may coordinate investigations with an in-house attorney. Also, HR may coordinate with the security department, especially if those departments contain staff with prior law enforcement background and training.

Another alternative is to ask an outside attorney to conduct the investigation. Although an expensive option, putting an attorney in charge of a workplace harassment investigation may show that the organization wants objectivity and is concerned about the seriousness of the charge. In the event the charge is against a senior member of management, utilizing outside attorneys may be the best strategy to avoid conflict of interest charges.

According to the Federal Trade Commission, employers that hire outside organizations to investigate harassment claims must follow Fair Credit Reporting Act (FCRA) procedures. The FTC believes that an outside firm performing a harassment investigation on behalf of an employer is a "consumer reporting agency." Therefore, the report would most likely be an "investigative consumer report." Violations requiring disciplinary action could reasonably be defined as an adverse employment decision. Therefore, if HR plans on hiring an outside party to conduct the harassment investigation, be sure to follow the FCRA rules. If unsure, consult with legal counsel for guidance.

Obtaining relevant information

HR must take quick action if it receives a complaint from an employee about improper workplace behavior. The goal of the investigation is to gather all relevant information to help determine whether improper behavior has occurred. HR needs to identify and obtain the information quickly.

What should HR be looking for? Consider any information that will help verify facts as well as help identify persons who should be interviewed and what questions should be asked. Review the personnel files of the complainant, the alleged harasser and any witnesses. Seek out relevant information throughout the investigation by repeatedly asking witnesses and anyone else involved whether or not they have any documentation that would be helpful in resolving the matter.

✓ *Checklist*

Relevant documents to review

Deborah Tjaden, founder of HR Management Solutions, Inc., suggested during a conference sponsored by the Council on Education in Management that HR professionals review the following documents when conducting an internal investigation:

☐ rules, policies, and procedures;
☐ memoranda or notes regarding the incident;

☐ time cards, logs or diaries;
☐ expense reports and receipts;
☐ communications to employees;
☐ prior complaints;
☐ personnel files and security files;
☐ manager's notes and files; and
☐ samples of the employee's work and others for comparison.

Conducting the interviews

The complainant

As explained above, when an employee first brings a complaint to HR or to a member of management, the person hearing the complaint for the first time must act as a "LEADER"—**L**isten, **E**ncourage, **A**sk questions, **D**ocument, **E**xplain and **R**espond.

Often, the person to whom a complaint is brought initially is not the same person who will conduct the investigation. Therefore, not all bases will necessarily be covered in that initial meeting. The following are some tips on interviewing the complaining employee ("the complainant") once an investigation into workplace harassment has begun. These tips are applicable either during the initial meeting or in a follow-up meeting once an investigator has been assigned.

1. Get details. Ask the employee for specific details regarding the alleged workplace harassment. Include questions regarding:
◆ the type of conduct and its frequency;
◆ what was said or done;
◆ where it occurred;
◆ the dates that the conduct occurred; and
◆ the time period over which the conduct occurred.

Find out whether or not there was a pattern of previous episodes; was the person bringing the complaint aware of similar behavior by the accused towards any other employee?

2. Understand the context. Get the specific context in which the conduct occurred, including the nature and general description of the work area and the specific location. Find out whether the conduct occurred at a work-related function, during working time, or after hours.

Also determine the time relationship between the occurrence of the alleged conduct, its effect on the complainant, and the time when the complainant made the report. If there was a time lag between the occurrence and the report, find out why the complainant waited before reporting the situation. A plausible explanation may be the employee's fear, either of retaliation or simple embarrassment.

It is helpful to prepare a detailed chronology. This will help you analyze whether there might have been certain events that trig-gered the complaint—for example, a denial of promotion, pay raise, or a transfer.

DON'T miss this

Find out if there are any witnesses or documents that may sup-port the claim. For example, ask about cards, letters, notes, voice mail messages, e-mail messages, expense reports, diaries, pictures or photographs.

3. Understand the impact. Determine the effect of the conduct on the complainant.

 ◆ Identify what harm the conduct caused (for example, were there financial or economic effects? Did the complainant miss work or visit the doctor? What about psychological effects like sleeplessness, loss of appetite, depression or anxiety?)
 ◆ Was the conduct received as a joke? Was it really unwelcome? Did it embarrass, frighten or humiliate the complainant?

Often, employees state that, while they may have acted as if they were not offended by harassment, they did so out of fear or because they felt threatened or intimidated. It is important for HR to remember that the real issue is whether the behavior was un-welcome. Probe gently to get as much information as possible.

DON'T miss this

4. Find out what the complainant wants. Try to find out how the employee wants the situation resolved. It may be hard for him or her to come up with a succinct answer; in fact, it's possible that the complainant has never considered that question. Probe further by finding out:

◆ Can the employee continue to work for or with the accused?
◆ Can the employee be productive?
◆ Will it be embarrassing or awkward for the employee, enough so that it will interfere with the employee's ability to do the job?
◆ Does the employee need counseling?

5. Explain the next steps. Explain that the charges are serious and that HR will conduct a thorough investigation before reaching any conclusions. Assure the employee that he or she will not be retaliated against for making the complaint.

WHAT you need to know

> Make *no* statements about the accused's character, job performance or family life, either to excuse or condemn the alleged behavior. If the accused were to sue for defamation, this might be enough evidence for a finding of "malice" or spitefulness. Malice wipes out the legal privilege that employers have to lawfully discuss these kinds of situations internally.

6. Get a written statement. Ask the employee to provide the details of the complaint in writing. If the employee is reluctant to write it down, don't argue, but make a note of the employee's reluctance. If the employee agrees to provide a written summary, attorney Lisa Lavelle Burke suggests that HR ask that it include:

◆ a list of all the employee's issues, concerns and complaints;
◆ the relevant facts and dates the employee believes support his or her concerns;
◆ the names of people the employee thinks may have information relevant to the investigation; and
◆ suggestions for obtaining relevant documentation (such as memos or performance reviews).

7. Summarize. Burke, speaking at a seminar co-sponsored by Patton Boggs, LLP, CCH INCORPORATED and the Society for Human Resource Management (SHRM), also suggested providing a memo or letter to the employee summarizing the issues raised. This document will provide both HR and the complaining employee an opportunity to make sure that all of the issues are clearly understood and that nothing has been left out. The confirmation memo should:

◆ identify the issues;
◆ identify the facts provided by the employee to support the issues;
◆ confirm these are all the issues raised;
◆ identify the person investigating the matter and confirm his or her impartiality and fairness;
◆ identify a roadmap for the investigation; and
◆ outline the employer's expectations for the employee raising the issue.

The accused

Once HR has met with the person who brought the complaint, it is time to meet with the person accused of inappropriate conduct ("the accused"). If there is more than one person who is accused of harassment, meet with each one individually rather than together.

1. Explain the reason for the meeting. Begin by telling the accused the purpose of the investigation. He or she may have no idea why the meeting was called. Provide enough information about the complaint so that the accused can know what he or she is responding to. Explain that a full, thorough investigation of the allegations will be conducted before any conclusions are reached. Assure the accused that confidentiality will be maintained to the fullest extent. Explain that disclosure of information about the complaint and investigation will be strictly limited to those with a legitimate need to know.

It is important that HR treat the accused party with respect and objectivity. Do not make assumptions about guilt based on prior history or simply on the fact that a complaint has been made. Conduct a complete investigation of the current situation.

2. Obtain a statement. As with the complainant, ask the accused for a written statement. HR usually has more leverage with the accused than with the complainant because of the potential disciplinary nature of the investigation. Again, if the accused refuses to provide a written statement, document that fact.

3. Identify the accused's relationship to the complainant. Was the accused a supervisory employee, a coworker or a nonemployee?

If the individual was a supervisor, indicate the individual's job title, obtain a copy of the individual's job description, and determine the individual's specific duties at the time of the alleged harassment.

- ◆ Determine whether the accused directed, or had responsibility for, the work of the complainant or other employees.
- ◆ Did he or she have authority to recommend employment decisions affecting others (for example, hiring, firing or promoting)?
- ◆ Was he or she responsible for maintaining or administrating the records of others?
- ◆ If sexual harassment is alleged, was there any prior consensual relationship between the parties?
- ◆ How long have the parties known each other?
- ◆ Is there a history of group or individual socializing?
- ◆ Is there any motive for the complainant to make false charges?

WHAT you need to know

> The employer is liable for the actions of supervisory employees or agents with immediate or successively higher authority over the victim, regardless of whether the acts were authorized or even forbidden by the employer, and regardless of whether the employer knew or should have known of their occurrence.

4. Consider how the accused reacts. You can expect the accused to deny the charges. Observe the reaction. Note whether or not there is surprise, anger or disbelief.

Describe the details of the complaint and pay attention to the areas of disagreement between each person's recollection of the events. If the accused denies the allegations, probe further to determine what he or she thinks are the reasons that could have motivated the employee to make the complaint. Determine if there are any facts to support the accused's side of the story.

WHAT you need to know

> If the person accused of harassment does not deny the conduct but explains the circumstances, there may be no need to investigate further. In this case, determine an appropriate response.

5. Gather more evidence. Find out if there are any witnesses, documentation or other evidence that can support the accused's denial of the allegations. When faced with a "he said, she said" claim, investigate further. If there are no witnesses to the alleged conduct, ask other employees if they have ever been subject to objectionable conduct but do not name the accused.

In addition to liability to harassment victims, employers could also be liable to harassers for inadequate or incomplete investigations. When employment decisions are based on workplace harassment investigations, good investigative practices must be used.

6. Caution against wrongdoing. Warn the accused that retaliation against the complainant is prohibited and can result in discipline, up to and including discharge. Caution the accused of the risk of personal defamation liability if he or she makes malicious or false statements or discusses the matter with others. It's important to stress these things in every case regardless of your personal belief as to whether or not the complaint was legitimate.

What if the accused wants a lawyer present? An alleged harasser is not entitled to attorney representation during investigatory interviews. But the accused should be reassured that:
- ◆ No conclusions have been reached;
- ◆ The investigations will be conducted fairly and objectively; and
- ◆ Confidentiality will be maintained to the fullest extent.

It is possible that the accused still might have legitimate concerns about the integrity of the process. If so, these concerns should be addressed immediately.

> Although the accused has no right to representation by a lawyer, he or she is probably entitled to have a union representative present if the company is unionized, or a coworker present if it is not.

Other witnesses

HR should interview *anyone* who has knowledge that will support or deny the complainant's allegations. If possible, obtain signed statements. Witness evidence is very critical to the investigation.

Without it, it is simply the complainant's word against that of the accused. Determine whether information provided by witnesses is based on firsthand knowledge of the facts, hearsay or gossip. And document unsuccessful attempts to interview persons who no longer work for the organization.

Be aware that often witnesses are reluctant to come forward out of fear of punishment or even of awkwardness among their fellow employees. Assure witnesses that their cooperation is important, that their testimony is confidential and that they will not be retaliated against for providing honest responses and information. Warn witnesses of the risk of personal defamation liability if they make malicious or false statements or discuss the matter with others.

Don't unnecessarily disclose information to witnesses. For example, instead of asking, "Did you see Ramel touch Sarita?" ask "Have you seen anyone touch Sarita at work in a way that made her feel uncomfortable?"

✓ Checklist

Interviewing the supervisor

When questioning the complainant's and accused's supervisor(s):

☐ Ask about any discipline problems and behavior patterns on the part of the accused or the complainant.

☐ Determine whether or not the supervisor had any knowledge of the relationship between the parties.

☐ Find out whether the complainant reported the conduct to the supervisor or if the supervisor was in a position to observe the conduct.

☐ Consider whether the supervisor should have been alerted to conduct. For example, was the conduct discussed in the presence of the supervisor, or were there any rumors circulating?

Determining credibility

What if there are no witnesses to the alleged harassment? Sexual and other unlawful harassment often happens in private with no witnesses. The resolution of a workplace harassment claim often depends upon the credibility of the parties. Unfortunately, these "he said she said" situations may be the rule and not the exception. How do you handle a situation where it comes down to weighing two different stories of what happened?

The EEOC and juries can find that workplace harassment occurred based solely on the victim's description of what happened. This means that the fact that there are no other witnesses does not *automatically* mean that the employer should take no action against the accused.

Consider the following in evaluating a "he said she said" situation. In order to find that the victim is believable, the EEOC gives great weight to a victim's ability to provide a sufficiently detailed and internally consistent account of the events. If the employee is unable to present any facts that support his or her story, the complaint will be perceived as less believable.

✔ ✔ ✔ *Checklist*

Factors to help determine whether harassment occurred

A general denial by the accused will carry little weight with the EEOC when other supporting evidence exists. HR should look for surrounding evidence to support or disprove a harassment claim. Such evidence may be found by asking the following questions:

- ☐ Do coworkers have any knowledge of the conduct?
- ☐ Did anyone observe the victim's behavior shortly after the alleged incident of harassment? The accused's behavior?
- ☐ Did the victim discuss the matter with another person such as a counselor, doctor or close friend?
- ☐ Did anyone notice any change in the victim's behavior at work or in the way that the alleged harasser treated the victim?
- ☐ Were other employees treated in a similar manner by the alleged harasser?

Documenting the process

A complete and accurate record can show that an employer promptly and thoroughly investigated a harassment complaint and that its resolution of the complaint was appropriate. Also, it can be invaluable in defending against a wrongful discharge or defamation lawsuit by a person found guilty of harassment.

Therefore, it is important to develop and keep accurate records of the particulars of a workplace harassment investigation.

◆ Take detailed notes during all interviews.

◆ Save all written statements submitted by the complainant, the accused and witnesses, as well as any other documentation or materials acquired during the investigation.

◆ Do not attempt to reach a legal conclusion in the documentation, but refer to violations of the employer's policy. For example, don't say that William sexually harassed Margo. Instead, say that William repeatedly asked Margo to date him over her stated objections, repeatedly made sexual comments to Margo, and repeatedly complained about his marital relations to Margo, again over her objections. Once you have specified the facts, you can then categorize it as inappropriate or unprofessional conduct according to your employer's policy.

WHAT you need to know

> Preserve the complete record in a safe, confidential manner for at least as long as may be required by any applicable regulatory or state statute of limitations.

Maintaining confidentiality

Once an investigation begins, the facts should be kept as confidential as possible and revealed only on a strict "need to know" basis. Don't promise complete confidentiality, either in the bias-free policy or during interviews. HR especially cannot promise the complaining employee that his or her identity will not ever be revealed. To fairly confront the alleged harasser, legal experts advise that HR must be able to say who complained or what the objectionable conduct was.

Everyone involved in the investigation—including the person making the report, the accused and witnesses—should be advised to keep investigatory discussions strictly confidential. Making sure that workplace harassment complaints and investigations are handled as confidentially as possible not only will encourage employees to come forward with their complaints, but will also reduce the risk of a defamation lawsuit.

Understanding and avoiding defamation

What is defamation? Defamation involves a false or malicious (intentionally harmful) statement, either written or spoken, about an employee that results in damage to the employee's reputation. Not only can an employer be faced with defamation liability based on statements made in connection with the investigation or resolution of a harassment complaint, so can the individuals who made the statements.

Truth is an absolute defense to defamation claims, but there is always the risk that the complaint and statements made during an investigation are false or exaggerated, or even that a finding of harassment is mistaken. Moreover, while a "qualified privilege" usually protects harassment investigators and witnesses who make defamatory statements, the privilege will be lost if the statements are recklessly or maliciously made, if they go beyond the scope of the investigation, or if they are made to someone who has no legitimate need to know about the matter.

✓ Checklist

Preventing defamation during a harassment investigation

Follow these tips to avoid the risk of defamation liability:

☐ Never discuss a workplace harassment complaint with anyone who does not have a legitimate need to receive the information.

☐ Make sure that all discussions of the matter are in a private area and cannot be overheard.

☐ Do not send e-mail or leave voice mail that discloses details of a workplace harassment complaint or investigation.

☐ Do not seek information or make statements concerning the parties that go beyond the scope of the investigation.

☐ Caution the accused, accuser and witnesses of the risk of personal defamation liability if they make spiteful or untrue statements during an investigation or discuss the matter with others.

☐ Do not draw any conclusions about the matter before all the facts are in.

☐ Develop a complete and accurate written record of all investigative interviews. When possible, obtain written statements.

☐ Make sure that the final determination is solidly based on the facts. Never describe the conduct as worse than it was.

☐ Keep confidential all records concerning a harassment investigation. Records should be kept in a separate confidential file, not in the accused's personnel file.

☐ Do not broadcast the results of the investigation as an example to others or as a training tool.

☐ If HR determines that a harassment complaint has merit, do not refer to the harasser's conduct as "workplace harassment." Rather, refer to it as unprofessional or inappropriate conduct. That way, if there is a policy against inappropriate conduct in place, HR may take necessary disciplinary action and still avoid the battle of determining whether the behavior at issue amounts to the unlawful harassment.

Protecting the accuser and the accused

Depending how severe the alleged harassment is, it may be necessary to take corrective action during the investigation. Doing so can serve to reduce the risk that the complainant will quit and/or take legal action, as well as help prevent liability if a lawsuit is filed.

✔ ✔ **Checklist**

Remedies for harassment during an investigation
Possible corrective actions include:

☐ Immediate removal of offensive graffiti or materials from the workplace.
☐ Temporarily transferring either the alleged harasser or the complainant (but heed the cautionary note below).
☐ Offering the complainant a paid leave of absence.
☐ Offering to pay for counseling for the complainant.
☐ Placing the alleged harasser on a nondisciplanary leave of absence.

Any job transfer during the investigation—of the complainant or the accused—must not disadvantage either party. Any perception that the reassignment is "less than" the current assignment can be interpreted as retaliation. It is generally a good idea to make reassignment offers dependent upon the approval of those involved. However, it is not required that corrective measures be those that the employee requests or prefers. What matters is that they are effective.

For example, Dimitri may ask that his coworkers be reassigned to less desirable positions that pay substantially less. Since this would obviously disadvantage the accused employees, it probably would be a bad idea to grant Dimitri's request. The better course of action would be to grant Dimitri a paid leave of absence until a full investigation into the matter has been completed.

The Quiz

1. If an employee reports that she is a victim of disability harassment but asks that HR not take any action because she wants her complaint to be kept strictly confidential, HR should:
   a. Do nothing as requested.
   b. Tell the employee that her complaint will be treated as confidentially as possible and begin the investigation process.
   c. Immediately transfer the complaining employee to a different department.

2. HR should not address a complaint of racial   ❑ True   ❑ False
   harassment that allegedly occurred several years ago.

3. A member of HR who sees that an employee has posted sexually explicit posters in his work area should:
   a. Handle the situation as if someone had complained.
   b. Do nothing. Since nobody has complained, it must not be a problem.
   c. Ask around to see if the posters offend anybody.

4. HR should request—but not require—a person   ❑ True   ❑ False
   who complains about workplace harassment
   to provide a written statement concerning the matter.

5. Keiko enters your office and requests that she be reassigned to a different department because her coworkers "act funny" around her and make her "nervous." What should you do?
   a. Tell Keiko that she needs to try harder to fit in and that she is welcome to come back and see you if the situation gets worse.
   b. Reassign Keiko to a less desirable position.
   c. Encourage Keiko to be more specific about what her coworkers are saying or doing that is making her nervous.

Answer key: 1.b, 2.F, 3.a, 4.T, 5.c

Resolution and corrective action

Making a determination 152

The hard-to-resolve claim 154

BEST PRACTICES: Solutions to
remedy the unsolvable complaint 155

Taking prompt action 156

BEST PRACTICES: Quick corrective action
excuses liability at trial 158

Notice of resolution 158

Addressing the victim 159

Transfers and reassignments 159

The false complaint 160

Disciplining the offender 160

Choose the proper discipline 160

BEST PRACTICES: Postal Service picks
suitable discipline for questionable conduct 160

Be consistent 161

Addressing the workforce 162

Preventing retaliation 162

Documenting the process 163

Following up 165

The Quiz 166

Ravi, a Hindi employee, has made a complaint to the HR office, stating that he has been the victim of ethnic harassment. You have investigated the complaint by reviewing relevant documents. You have also interviewed Ravi and the two coworkers he accused of harassment, Colin and Joe. In addition, you have interviewed their supervisor, Renee, and the other coworker in the group, Juanita. In short, the interviews went as follows.

Ravi was believable and gave a detailed description of his side of the story. He accused Colin and Joe of making off-color jokes about his ethnic background. He reported feeling isolated from his group and unable to perform as well as his coworkers.

Colin and Joe denied acting in a harassing or discriminatory manner. They both admitted that they had made ethnic jokes, but claimed that Ravi participated by making jokes about their ethnic backgrounds—Irish and Italian. They claimed that it was all in good fun and that they had no idea that Ravi was offended. Renee had no knowledge of inappropriate comments by Colin or Joe—to Ravi or anyone else in the workplace. She has noticed that Ravi has been "keeping to himself" and has been taking a lot of time off lately.

Juanita recalled several times when Colin and Joe "teased" Ravi about not being a "true American." She also remembered one time when she heard Colin call Ravi a "smelly camel rider." That time Ravi walked away and didn't return to the work area for several minutes. Juanita didn't recall Ravi ever commenting about Colin's or Joe's ethnicity. Have Colin and Joe engaged in inappropriate conduct? What should HR do?

Making a determination

Once HR has thoroughly investigated potential harassment, the next step is to make a determination as to:

1. Whether violation of the bias-free policy occurred, and
2. What action will be taken based on the findings.

Attempting to resolve a complaint to the satisfaction of all concerned (to the extent possible and reasonable) should be HR's main objective. Whatever the result, it is important to ensure that any determination is well founded and solidly supported by facts in the investigative record.

Companies responding to a 1999 survey by the Society for Human Resource Management (SHRM) revealed that, after investigation, two out of three (65 percent) sexual harassment complaints were substantiated. Those complaints that were substantiated resulted in a warning (29 percent) or some form of disciplinary action against the alleged harassers.

DON'T miss this

HR's decision about what to do may not be completely satisfactory to the complaining employee. One reason may be that the employee does not fully understand HR's desire to resolve the situation to everyone's satisfaction. Therefore, it is important that the complaining employee understand that HR is taking the appropriate steps.

✓ Checklist

Counseling the complaining employee

To help the employee accept HR's decision and get past the troubling situation, follow these steps:

☐ Give the employee making the complaint someone to talk to who will be sympathetic and credible to the employee.

☐ Help the employee understand what is and is not workplace harassment.

☐ Explain why HR has made the determination that it has and what it hopes to accomplish.

☐ Probe to be sure that the employee making the complaint feels secure about the immediate future.

☐ If the employee making the complaint fears further harassment, explain what he or she should do about it given the situation.

The hard-to-resolve claim

Workplace harassment is an especially difficult area for one primary reason. HR may do everything right, but it still may be impossible to determine whether workplace harassment has occurred. HR may adopt a strong policy against harassment. It may conduct training about workplace harassment. An effective procedure for making workplace harassment complaints may be in place. Yet, when an actual complaint is placed before HR, conflicting evidence may make it impossible to establish firmly that workplace harassment has or has not occurred.

This happens most often in what is sometimes referred to as the "he said, she said" situation. The victim of the claimed harassment might make a complaint like this about a coworker: "He made off-color jokes I was supposed to laugh at, stared provocatively at me, and brushed himself against me on several occasions."

When HR questions the accused harasser, however, he may declare with great certainty and apparent honesty, "Yes, I made off-color jokes, but I was careful. I watched to see how she was taking them, and she always seemed to smile. But that's all I did; I never 'stared' at her, and I certainly didn't 'brush myself against her.'"

What is HR looking at in a case like this? If both employees stick to their stories—"He's harassed me" and "No, I haven't"—and there are no witnesses, HR may never know what actually occurred.

Bring closure. Even in these difficult situations, it is important for HR to bring closure. HR does know that a complaint of harassment has been made. Even if you can't determine what actually happened, it is important that the complaint be resolved. HR should bring the complaint to some formal conclusion through investigation and communication with all parties involved. The steps in the process and the final resolution should be documented.

At the very least, HR should:

◆ Reemphasize to all parties involved in the complaint the employer's prohibition of harassment and discrimination in the workplace.

◆ Document that a complaint was received and an investigation took place, but that it could not be determined if inappropriate conduct actually occurred.

◆ Reassure the complaining employee that his or her employment conditions will not be adversely affected by the complaint and urge him or her to immediately report any future incidents of workplace harassment.

> If the complaint can't be proven either way, do not discipline either the alleged harasser or the victim.

**WHAT
you need
to know**

Of course, there is no guarantee that the victim will not take the complaint elsewhere—such as to a lawyer or even to the EEOC. But taking steps to resolve the complaint will put HR in a much better position to explain the organization's position should the need ever arise.

Best Practices

Solutions to remedy the unsolvable complaint

Legal experts at Jackson Lewis, a national employment law firm representing management, suggest that where the results of an investigation do not clearly suggest whether harassment has occurred, HR's best ally in fashioning a response may be the complaining employee. Continued communication with that employee regarding the outcome of the investigation and the action he or she would like taken in order to continue working comfortably often helps bring an otherwise inconclusive investigation to a close. Jackson Lewis suggests the following actions:

◆ Notify the complaining employee that after an investigation, his or her claims could not be substantiated.

◆ Thank the employee for coming forward and provide assurances of the employer's commitment to providing a work environment free of harassment.

◆ Tell the employee that the accused has been reminded of the employer's intolerance of any type of harassment.

◆ Encourage the employee to immediately report any further incidents of harassment. Reassure the accused that because the investigation proved inconclusive, he or she will suffer no punishment.

◆ Warn the accused that any subsequent allegations might result in more severe discipline.

◆ Remind the accused of the employer's anti-harassment policy and the penalties for violating it.

If the complaining employee is not satisfied with this response, other options may be available. For example, is it possible to transfer one of the workers or to alter work schedules so they no longer work together?

If possible, these options should be made available so that it is clear that the organization is doing all that it can to resolve the situation to everyone's satisfaction. If separating the two workers is not possible, providing the entire department with additional training may be an appropriate solution.

Taking prompt action

HR must take prompt action when harassment or other inappropriate conduct is found. This means immediately doing whatever is necessary to stop the behavior.

WHAT you need to know

Why is it so important that the action be prompt? Any delay in stopping known harassment sharply increases an employer's risk of liability should the victim decide to sue. Moreover, by acting promptly, the organization sends a clear message to the workforce that harassment and other forms of inappropriate conduct will not be tolerated.

✓ ✓ *Checklist*

Types of corrective action include:

☐ An apology for an unintended remark.

☐ Disciplinary action, which may include a warning, reprimand, suspension, or even discharge. The discipline should reflect the severity of the conduct.

☐ Training for the accused about the inappropriate behavior and the employer's bias-free policy.

☐ Monitoring of the accused to be certain that the harassment stops.

☐ Restoration of any job benefits or opportunities to the victim that were lost because of the harassment.

☐ Appropriate counseling or other compensation for losses.

☐ Expunging any negative evaluations in the employee's personnel file that arose from the harassment.

☐ Additional training about appropriate workplace behavior.

The actions taken should be designed to correct the behavior and to prevent it from happening again. The overall goal should be to place the employee who complained in the position that he or she would have been in if the misconduct had never occurred.

If an employee files an EEOC charge, what does the EEOC look for in terms of actions by the employer? The EEOC looks to see if an the employer did several key things, said EEOC senior trial attorney June Wallace Carson during the 2000 Technical Assistance Program Seminar in Lincolnshire, Illinois:

WHAT you need to know

◆ What, if anything, did the employer do in response to the employee's complaint?

◆ Was the action taken appropriate to the circumstances?

◆ Was the action taken effective?

◆ Was the harassing conduct eliminated and was the victim made whole?

Consider Ravi's situation. It appears that Colin and Joe did make derogatory statements to Ravi about his ethnic heritage. While the behavior may or may not violate federal law, it is inappropriate and must be stopped. Colin and Joe should be disciplined and monitored to make sure the behavior does not continue. Anti-harassment training is surely in order, at least for Colin and Joe; possibly for the entire workforce. To help Ravi return to a comfortable work environment, HR should offer counseling services. It may also be necessary to compensate him for any unpaid time he took away from work due to stress caused by the inappropriate behavior.

A⁺ *Best Practices*

Quick corrective action excuses liability at trial

A court ruled that an employer's immediate and appropriate corrective action excused the employer from sexual harassment liability under federal law. In this case, an employee complained to her employer that her coworker had talked to her about sexual activities and touched her in an offensive manner. Within four days of receiving the complaint, the employer did the following:

◆ investigated the charges;
◆ reprimanded the guilty employee;
◆ placed him on probation; and
◆ warned him that further misconduct would result in discharge.

A second coworker who had witnessed the harassment was also reprimanded for not intervening on the victim's behalf or reporting the conduct.

Notice of resolution

Once the investigation has been completed, those who were involved should be told the results of the investigation and whether or not corrective action was taken. Usually the person who reported the conduct should not be told the particulars of any disciplinary action, other than that the employer has acted appropriately.

Addressing the victim

Once HR determines that harassment or other inappropriate behavior occurred, it must take action that will ensure that the victim is no longer subject to the wrongful behavior.

Depending on the circumstances, it may be enough to counsel the harasser and arrange for an apology. Or, if the conduct was more severe, HR may need to arrange for a transfer or reassignment (see below). In some cases it may be appropriate to offer counseling services to overcome the stress caused by the harassment. This may be a good time to offer the company's EAP services, if available.

HR must also address the victim's needs by restoring any job benefits or opportunities that may have been lost because of the harassment. This may include compensation for any lost pay or sick days used because of the stress of the harassment. It may also be necessary for HR to expunge negative comments from a performance review tainted by a harassing supervisor's motives.

If someone with supervisory authority was the harasser, it is critical that HR check to ensure that no negative job actions were taken for unlawful reasons. If they were, HR must take action to reverse the actions as quickly as possible.

Transfers and reassignments

In some cases it may be appropriate for HR to separate the victim and the harasser. Exercise extreme caution in this area. Any transfer must not appear to disadvantage the person making the harassment complaint. If the person making the complaint is reassigned, for example, to a less desirable position or to a position with few promotion opportunities, the employer may be seen as retaliating against the person for making a complaint.

◆ When attempting to remedy harassment, avoid requiring that the complaining employee work less desirable hours or in a less desirable location.

◆ If HR offers to transfer the complaining employee, try to get his or her consent and make sure the transfer position is substantially similar to his or her prior position.

The false complaint

What if harassment allegations turn out to be false? It is important for HR to determine whether the person deliberately lied or simply misperceived the conduct alleged to be workplace harassment. Discipline of someone who mistakenly reported harassment not only can discourage employees from making complaints, but can also result in liability for retaliation. Don't impose discipline on the complaining party unless you are absolutely certain that the person was fully aware of the falsity of the claim at the time the person made it. If discipline is warranted, it should be consistent with that imposed for dishonesty in comparable circumstances.

Disciplining the offender

Choose the proper discipline

If harassment is found, HR must decide how to appropriately discipline the offending supervisor or employee who was responsible for the harassment. When imposing discipline, consider the severity, past history, frequency and pervasiveness of the conduct.

Appropriate forms of discipline can include oral or written warnings, reprimands, demotion, suspension and probation. If the conduct is very offensive or if the harasser's ability to perform is very impaired, discharge may be the only alternative. Lesser discipline should be accompanied with a warning that any similar misconduct in the future will result in immediate discharge.

A+ Best Practices

Postal Service picks suitable discipline for questionable conduct

The US Postal Service avoided liability for sexual harassment because it took appropriate corrective action by disciplining a male coworker found to have sexually harassed a female employee. The Postal Service learned of the alleged harasser's questionable conduct when another employee reported having seen the accused grab the female employee's hand with the intention of kissing it and refusing to let go despite her protests. Management investigated within three days of the report and the accused's supervisor reprimanded his conduct and warned him on two occasions to stay away from the female employee. Because the employee found the male employee's presence discomforting, management also moved her to a different job farther away from his area.

The victim argued to a court that the Postal Service should have disciplined the male employee more extensively. But the court disagreed. It viewed the admonishments as adequate discipline given that there were 16 reported incidents of harassing behavior, none of which were severe and pervasive enough to create a hostile working environment. The discipline given, along with the removal of the female employee from the work area, stopped the harassment altogether and therefore was sufficient.

Be consistent

HR must make sure that all actions taken for violation of policy are not only timely, but also consistent. Sometimes employees who have been disciplined or terminated for workplace harassment will later claim that they were unlawfully discriminated against because of their sex, race, age or other protected characteristic. In other words, they say that they were treated differently from other employees accused of workplace harassment.

Therefore, before disciplining or discharging an employee accused of workplace harassment, you should carefully consider how the organization has treated other workers accused of similar behavior. To assist with this review, HR should maintain confidential records regarding harassment investigations and claims.

If HR decides to change past procedures, be careful to evaluate any ramifications and consider how you will handle any behavior that occurred before the change was officially made. Remember, it is important that any disciplinary action be taken without regard to sex, age, race or any other protected status.

WHAT you need to know

Addressing the workforce

HR may need to take additional corrective action that will persuade potential harassers to refrain from unlawful harassment. Some actions that may be taken include:

◆ Conduct refresher harassment training for all employees and supervisory personnel.

◆ Establish front-line recognition of what harassment is. Use examples; elaborate so that the message is clear.

◆ Eliminate a climate that encourages harassment. Discourage swearing, off-color jokes, and after-work socializing that includes heavy drinking. Emphasize the importance of setting the same high standard of conduct outside of the workplace, such as during business trips.

◆ Redistribute the bias-free policy. Make sure the policy contains all necessary elements, including effective complaint procedures.

Preventing retaliation

Failure to stop reprisals against an employee who complains of harassment or someone who participates in a workplace harassment investigation can result in liability for an employer, regardless of the outcome of the investigation. Federal law prohibits such retaliation. An employer can be held liable not only for retaliatory actions by managers and supervisors but also for those by coworkers. Just as an employer must promptly and effectively stop harassment, it must do the same with respect to retaliatory activity.

✓ **Checklist**
✓

Steps for addressing retaliation

HR should prepare and respond to possible retaliation by:

☐ Encouraging the person who reported harassment, as well as workers who participate in the investigation, to let HR or a member of management know immediately if the behavior continues or if there are any further problems.

☐ Having someone continue to monitor the situation in order to ensure that the alleged harasser does not engage in retaliatory or other inappropriate conduct.
☐ Immediately stopping any conduct that appears to be retaliation.
☐ Counseling employees suspected or accused of retaliation about what retaliation is and the consequences for engaging in such action.
☐ After stopping retaliation, following up to ensure it does not resume.

Typically, very severe penalties including discharge are applied to individuals who retaliate, especially after having been warned not to do so in the course of an investigation. Additional corrective actions should be considered such as meetings, statements and training focusing on retaliation and the employer's strict prohibition.

What is retaliation?

Some of the most obvious types of unlawful retaliation are denial of promotion, denial of job benefits, demotion, suspension and discharge. Retaliation may also take the form of threats, reprimands, negative evaluations, and harassment.

Unlawful retaliation can occur even after the employment relationship ends. For example, a negative job reference may be viewed by a court as retaliatory if the reason the bad reference was provided was to "punish" the worker for having participated in an EEOC investigation.

WHAT you need to know

Documenting the process

It is crucial that HR record what was said during the investigation and what was done in response. Documentation is important to ensure that, down the road, other HR members are able to acquire the knowledge of the investigation. Documentation is also important in case an EEOC charge or lawsuit is brought against the organization. The employer's documents are often at the heart of such disputes.

Keeping records of complaints also allows HR to review for possible patterns of harassment by the same individual.

Document facts, not conclusions. Characterizations, adjectives and adverbs should be used sparingly, if at all. The goal is to document what people have actually said or done.

For example, don't document that "Raj said Marissa was upset by Steve's rude behavior." Instead record that "Raj heard Steve tell Marissa in a loud voice, 'you don't belong in a man's job and should be home taking care of your husband and family,'" and that "within a few minutes of hearing this comment, Raj saw Marissa begin to cry and leave the room."

✓✓ Checklist

What should you put in the file?

Legal experts at the Jackson Lewis law firm advise that HR place the following in the investigation file:

☐ The employee's complaint and any other documents and notes taken during the investigation;

☐ The employer's policy statements, including notices and handbook statements;

☐ The original written plan of who will be interviewed and list of topics to be addressed in the interviews;

☐ A summary of the investigative findings and the conclusions drawn; and

☐ Details concerning the corrective action taken and the reasons for taking it.

Documentation of the investigative process should not be placed in either the harasser or the harassed employee's personnel files, unless it is determined that inappropriate conduct occurred and that discipline is necessary.

Following up

Follow up is necessary to make sure that the remedy has been effective to stop the harassment and that no retaliation has been taken against the victim or witnesses. If the remedy has been ineffective, it may be necessary to increase the level of discipline. HR's failure to follow up can result in liability if harassment continues.

Worst case scenario

After Joyce's first complaint of sexual harassment by a male coworker, management informed the coworker that his conduct must stop and warned him that discipline would result if the conduct resumed. But Joyce subsequently reported repeated instances of harassment by the coworker. Management responded by adjusting the employees' shifts to reduce contact between them and by counseling the coworker and issuing additional oral warnings to him. Still, the harassment continued. The coworker was never reprimanded, issued a written warning, or disciplined in any manner. Joyce took her claim to court and won. The court said that although management took corrective action, the employer was still liable because its actions were not reasonably designed to end the harassment.

Solution. HR must follow up to make sure that harassment stops or the employer will face legal liability if the behavior continues. If a lesser degree of discipline has been ineffective, it may be necessary to take more severe measures to end workplace harassment.

?The Quiz

1. If HR decides to transfer a victim of harassment in order to ensure that the behavior stops, it should:
   a. Avoid requiring that the victim work less desirable hours or in a less desirable location.
   b. Try to get the victim's consent.
   c. Make sure that the transfer position is substantially similar to the victim's prior position.
   d. All of the above.

2. Any delay in stopping known harassment sharply increases an employer's risk of liability should the victim decide to sue.   ❑ True   ❑ False

3. If HR investigates a complaint of harassment and determines that inappropriate conduct did not occur, HR should:
   a. Immediately discipline the person who made complaint.
   b. Determine whether the person deliberately lied or simply misperceived the conduct alleged to be workplace harassment.
   c. Do nothing.

4. There is no need to increase the level of discipline imposed upon a harasser unless the victim makes another complaint.   ❑ True   ❑ False

Answer Key: 1.d, 2.T, 3.b, 4.F.

Diversity initiatives

Diversity overview.. **168**

    Why manage diversity? **169**

    Diversity vs. anti-harassment efforts **171**

    BEST PRACTICES: ABB powers up diversity effort.............. **172**

    Prevalence of diversity programs **173**

    The business case.. **175**

Focus of diversity initiatives **175**

    Race **176**

    Gender.. **177**

    Age **178**

    Religion... **178**

    Disability **179**

Diversity training **180**

    What type of training to offer? **180**

    Designing the program **181**

Maximizing the values of diversity... **183**

    Plan ahead **183**

    BEST PRACTICES: EEOC recommends
the "SPLENDID" approach... **183**

    Research... **184**

The Quiz.. **185**

In the past several years, the cultural make up of your organization has changed quite a bit. There are more women and persons of color in the workforce than ever before. You've also noticed a rise in the numbers of workers from diverse ethnic and religious backgrounds. You have seen to it that your organization has in place a strong program prohibiting unlawful discrimination and harassment—including a clear policy, comprehensive complaint system, and mandatory training for managers and employees. In fact, there are not any pressing EEO concerns—there have been no complaints of harassment or observations of inappropriate behavior. But you're starting to wonder whether your organization needs to do more to ensure the success of its culturally diverse workforce. Is it enough to communicate zero tolerance for harassment and require equal treatment? How are diversity programs different from anti-harassment and EEO programs?

Diversity overview

Does it seem like the term "diversity" often comes up whenever you read or hear about harassment and discrimination in the workplace? But what exactly does it mean for an employer to promote diversity?

WHAT you need to know

> The term "diversity" is often confused with the concept of preventing discrimination and harassment. But harassment prevention and diversity promotion are not the same thing (although a well-managed, culturally diverse workforce is less likely to have EEO problems).

For HR to manage cultural diversity means to assimilate various values and differences in the workforce. It means more than recruiting minority individuals to comply with EEO or affirmative action policies. It even means more than having a workforce with people of different cultural and ethnic backgrounds. Managing diversity also includes:

◆ *unifying* the diverse workforce;

◆ *recognizing* the differences of each member;

◆ *valuing* the different ideas they can bring to the organization; and

◆ *realizing* how those differences, when allowed to coexist in a positive atmosphere, can make the workforce *more productive* and can *increase morale.*

Why manage diversity?

Why should HR care about diversity, as long as the work environment is free from harassment and discrimination? Isn't it enough that there have been no complaints of harassment or observations of inappropriate behavior?

HR should care because as discriminatory barriers are broken, and the workforce continues to diversify, employers will have to take their anti-harassment and EEO policies a step further to remain competitive and to ensure that they have the best applicants and workers who are performing to their potential. Not only will employers need to hire members of different racial, ethnic, cultural, religious, gender and age groups, but they will have to find a way to honor their different values, expectations and capabilities and forge them into one team focused on the employers' goals. As you can see, although a good start, it very well may not be enough to communicate zero tolerance for harassment and require equal treatment.

✓ ✓ Checklist

EEOC's "best" practices in diversity programs

☐ Conduct training programs for all employees in EEO rights and responsibilities including, but not limited to:

- ◆ gender awareness;
- ◆ diversity;
- ◆ disability, pregnancy, and religious accommodation;
- ◆ harassment prevention; and
- ◆ affirmative action.

☐ Encourage and support formation of employee groups along diversity lines (*e.g.*, women, men, minorities, persons with disabilities, older persons, religious persons) to actively participate within the company in EEO matters.

☐ Form a Diversity Council with representatives of all interested organizations to discuss matters of equal employment opportunity.

☐ Encourage high-level management participation and interaction with employees and employee groups, and ensure employee access to management.

☐ Consider special emphasis programs and other events recognizing and highlighting the contributions of various cultural and/or social heritages.

☐ Publish a pamphlet or handbook detailing EEO rights and responsibilities, as well as diversity and affirmative action programs.

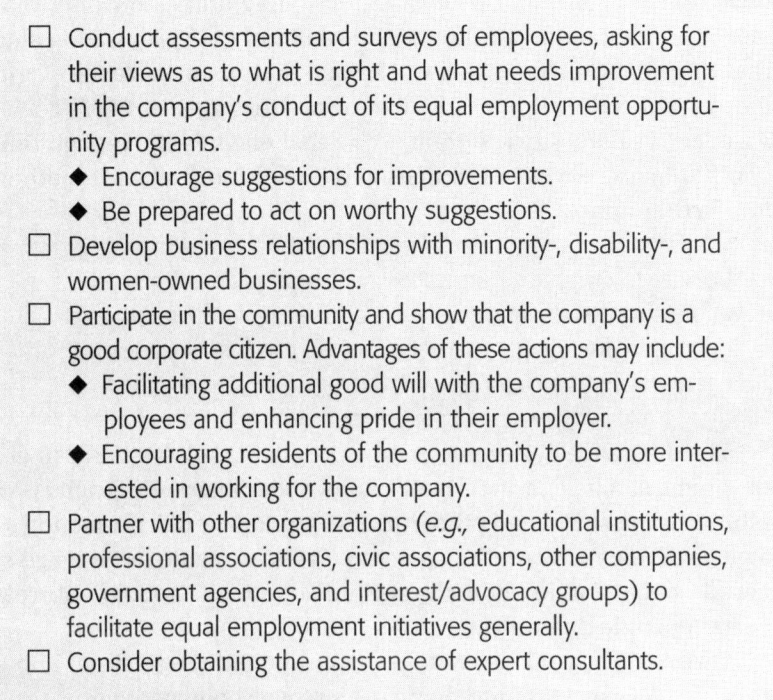

☐ Conduct assessments and surveys of employees, asking for their views as to what is right and what needs improvement in the company's conduct of its equal employment opportunity programs.
  ◆ Encourage suggestions for improvements.
  ◆ Be prepared to act on worthy suggestions.
☐ Develop business relationships with minority-, disability-, and women-owned businesses.
☐ Participate in the community and show that the company is a good corporate citizen. Advantages of these actions may include:
  ◆ Facilitating additional good will with the company's employees and enhancing pride in their employer.
  ◆ Encouraging residents of the community to be more interested in working for the company.
☐ Partner with other organizations (*e.g.*, educational institutions, professional associations, civic associations, other companies, government agencies, and interest/advocacy groups) to facilitate equal employment initiatives generally.
☐ Consider obtaining the assistance of expert consultants.

The practice of managing diversity raises many issues for the HR practitioner, far too many to sufficiently cover in one chapter. So what this Chapter aims to do is to provide a basic understanding of diversity principals so that you can better understand how your organization's diversity efforts will fit within the overall scheme of preventing harassment and discrimination.

Diversity vs. anti-harassment efforts

How can a cultural diversity policy that encourages HR, managers and employees to recognize the differences in various ethnic, age and gender groups coexist with the anti-discrimination laws that forbid employers from treating employees differently based on the differences in those very same categories? While it can sometimes seem confusing, the key is to focus on individuals.

A diversity program can be seen as a way to go beyond harassment prevention into a deeper commitment to draw from the entire workforce to get the most qualified applicants and to develop them into an optimally functioning unit. But doing that means understanding the needs and values of each group and using that information to create a workplace that helps to develop and motivate each individual to strive toward the organization's goals. An effective diversity program is one that ensures the recognition of differences moves individuals in the workforce closer together, not farther apart.

WHAT you need to know

> Be sure to emphasize education, which plays an integral part in the successful implementation of diversity in the workplace. Education discourages stereotyping and can foster respect for customs of other cultures.

The difference between diversity programs and anti-harassment programs can be characterized as one of emphasis. Programs prohibiting harassment and other forms of workplace discrimination as a general rule focus on things *not to do*—such as do not engage in certain behavior, do not make certain comments, and do not treat certain people differently.

On the other hand, diversity programs provide suggestions about things *to do*—such as participate in employee holiday programs and festivals, join employee groups and engage in mentoring.

Best Practices

ABB powers up diversity effort

Attracting and retaining a culturally diverse workforce tops the list of HR challenges for ABB Alstom Power, reports J. Vernon Glenn, Executive Advisor of Human Resources for the company's US power generation division. As part of its diversity program, the company has developed a wide variety of initiatives to encourage communication and foster diversity at its two Richmond facilities. Among its many programs and activities are:

All-associates meetings. Several times a year, the Turbine Generator Division president holds an all-associates meeting. The president provides all the facilities' associates with an update on what is going on in the company and what is going on in the world as it relates to the company. Associates are given the opportunity to ask questions and be heard.

Interview skills training. All managers and professionals who are involved in interviewing must attend detailed interview skills training.

Orientation training. All new hires and transfers attend a one-to-two hour orientation session in which they learn not only what their job responsibilities are, but also what it means from a legal standpoint for the company to be based in the United States. This includes an understanding of the company's affirmative action obligations.

International Diversity Month. This event provides associates an opportunity to talk about their diverse backgrounds and cultural heritage, including their language, traditions and foods.

Other cultural activities. The company strives to engage in cultural activities throughout the year, including Black History Month and a company-sponsored picnic called "Octoberfest."

Family activities. To maintain a family-friendly environment and promote open communication, the company sponsors picnics for workers and their families.

Prevalence of diversity programs

According to a 2000 survey by William M. Mercer, workplace diversity programs are in place in 67 percent of large organizations (5,000 or more employees) and in 24 percent of mid-size organizations (under 5,000 employees). While most large employers have workplace diversity programs, management support varies. *(Fax Facts Survey on Workforce Diversity).*

Most of the diversity programs were created in the last five to eight years. Survey respondents that didn't yet have a diversity program in place indicated that they had one under development (18 percent) or in the planning stage (23 percent).

Program success. When asked about the success of their diversity programs, respondents rated them about average or 5.3 on a scale of one (failure) to 10 (full success). Only 6 percent rate their efforts as highly successful (9 to 10 on the scale).

✔ *Checklist*

Most common diversity initiatives

At organizations surveyed in 2001 by the Society for Human Resource Management (SHRM) and FORTUNE magazine, diversity initiatives ranged from the simple to the complex. Respondents were asked if their organizations were involved with 15 different initiatives.

☐ Recruiting efforts designed to help increase diversity within the organization (75%).

☐ Diversity training initiatives, education and/or awareness efforts (66%).

☐ Community outreach related to diversity (61%).

☐ Diversity-related career development, such as mentoring (39%).

☐ Celebrating different cultural events, such as Black History Month or Heritage Month (38%).

☐ Measuring the management of diversity when evaluating the performance of managers (34%).

☐ Support groups (24%).

☐ Bilingual training for managers and employees (22%).

☐ Explicit promotion opportunities to break through glass ceiling (20%).

☐ Cultural orientation programs (19%).

☐ Training in English as a second language (19%).

☐ Use of symbols to promote diversity, such as logos or slogans (17%).

☐ Diversity-related conflict resolution (16%).

☐ Employer-paid literacy training (11%).

☐ Very informal efforts, nothing structured at all (19%).

The business case

The 2001 SHRM/FORTUNE magazine diversity survey found that top companies think diversity initiatives have a direct impact on the bottom line and help an organization keep a competitive edge. Specifically,

◆ 79 percent said a focus on diversity improves corporate culture;

◆ 77 percent said it improves recruitment of new employees; and

◆ 52 percent cited improved client relations.

The majority of HR professionals responding to the survey (91 percent) also said their diversity initiative helps their organization keep a competitive advantage. More than three-fourths said such initiatives do this by both improving corporate culture (83 percent) and improving employee morale (79 percent). More than half said it decreases interpersonal conflict among employees (58 percent), increases creativity (59 percent), and increases productivity (52 percent). In addition, 41 percent noted higher employee retention and a similar percentage cited decreased complaints and litigation.

Focus of diversity initiatives

Nearly all (96 percent) of the respondents to the SHRM/FORTUNE magazine survey said that their initiatives include race as an aspect of diversity and 88 percent cover gender. More than half said they also cover age (65 percent), disability (64 percent) and sexual orientation (57 percent). In addition, 11 percent indicated that their organizations covered other aspects of diversity, including thinking styles and patterns, marital status, seniority, education, socioeconomic status, merging company cultures and management and union relationships.

The William M. Mercer diversity survey received similar results. Of those companies with diversity programs in place, the following are addressed:

◆ Race (94%).

◆ Gender (90%).

◆ Disability (77%).

◆ Age (73%).

◆ Sexual orientation (58%).

Race

One of the more visible forms of workforce diversity is the integration of people of different racial backgrounds. While larger numbers of minority racial groups are entering the workforce, there are incidents where it does not appear that they are being given equal opportunity, much less involved in diversity initiatives. In response, many employers are making concerted efforts to track high-potential minorities and develop them with the intention of placing them in positions of management and decision-making authority.

✔ **Checklist**

Racial diversity initiatives
Here are some suggestions for better inclusion of members of racial groups:

☐ Be sure any pictures in organizational publications include all racial groups represented in the workforce (for example, pictures contained in annual reports, in-house communications and advertisements).

☐ Ensure all employee teams and committees include members of every racial group represented in the workforce.

☐ Provide support programs and mentors for trainees and individuals on fast track programs. Be sure there are role models that include members of diverse racial groups.

☐ Underscore the importance of diversity in generating profits. Examples of this emphasis should be found in mission and vision statements, training classes, executive management statements, diversity programs and monitoring.

☐ Sponsor employee events that include celebrations of all events, including those based in African American culture and other racial/ethnic groups.

☐ Have zero tolerance for discrimination. Any incident should be immediately investigated, and if the charges are founded, parties should be disciplined appropriately.

Gender

Gender diversity issues are similar to those of harassment and discrimination, but differ in that the focus is on the value of women in the workforce, including the creation of an environment that supports a balance of work and family. Two issues that often arise in the context of gender diversity are the presence of a glass ceiling and the lack of family-friendly programs.

Glass ceiling. "Glass ceiling" is a term that has come to mean the presence of discrimination at the higher management and professional levels within organizations. This concept implicitly recognizes that women have been employed in great numbers; however, senior level jobs are still filled by males. The concept is often cited as a fundamental workplace problem for certain racial groups as well, such as African Americans and Hispanics.

In addition to the relatively few women in executive roles (compared to lower ranks), there have also been several high-profile female executives that have either left their positions in order to devote more time to personal issues, or who have publicly stated that the tradeoff for success at a senior level is one that for them included not having children and marrying later than the norm. These women argue that the rules are the same for men and women—the opportunity to achieve executive status in a highly competitive environment requires total dedication and an almost total time commitment. They stress that no one can "have it all."

Family-friendly programs. Traditionally, women have been viewed as caretakers. Some organizations have proactively tried to encourage and enable women (and increasingly men as well) to remain in the workforce by recognizing their family obligations and taking steps to assist them in the form of on-site child care and flexible working hours.

Many proponents of gender diversity suggest that women contribute something different and important to the workplace and that the presence of representative numbers of women in the workplace demonstrates a commitment by the employer to the value of women in the workforce.

DON'T
miss
this

Age

Employers are facing increasing challenges as a result of the increasing age diversity in the workplace. With advances in medical technology and the aging of the baby boomer generation, management must now consider how to:

- best utilize older workers (born before 1940);
- accommodate the huge number of baby boomers (born 1946-1964) who are moving into a stage where promotion is expected and few spots exist; and
- motivate the newest generation of workers coming on the scene—Generation X and Generation Y (those born after 1964).

To manage age diversity, it is imperative to develop a spirit of interdependence between younger and older workers. This approach is less likely to result in division along age lines in the workforce.

WHAT you need to know

A program that has proved to be successful in using the potential of older workers is mentoring. While the program is not restricted by age, it arranges for an experienced worker to put his or her knowledge to work in guiding much less experienced employees. The result is a better-trained employee and increased motivation for both parties.

Religion

America is increasingly becoming a religiously diverse country. Muslim and Buddhist temples and affiliations are common in many cities and communities in addition to places of worship representative of the country's Judeo-Christian history. Increasingly, employees are demanding the freedom to speak and practice the tenets of their religion in the workplace. Valuing religion without sanctioning a specific religion is the key to balancing religious diversity in the workplace.

DON'T miss this

A 2001 survey by the Society for Human Resource Management (SHRM) and the Tanenbaum Center for Interreligious Understanding shows that religious diversity is growing in the workplace. More than one-third of participants (36 percent) reported that there are more religions represented in their workforces compared to five years ago. Increases were most prevalent in the high-tech and transportation industries.

Religious diversity is difficult to achieve because it relates to the morals and beliefs that an employee holds, which may come into direct conflict with those of the employer or other employees. As with other types of diversity, the best approach is to educate the workforce to be sensitive to the beliefs of others and to avoid stereotyping. This may mean stressing that the employer, as an organization, does not espouse one belief system over another.

Employers may be required to accommodate religious diversity, such as by:

◆ observing religious holidays;

◆ allowing prayers breaks; and

◆ accommodating dietary requirements or dress and grooming habits, and religiously motivated objections to training programs, patriotic programs and national holidays.

In setting dress and appearance policy, HR should take religious requirements into consideration when dealing with headwear (for example, hats, yarmulkes, headscarves and turbans) and physical appearance generally (for example, length of hair and beards).

DON'T
miss
this

Disability

The Americans with Disabilities Act is breaking down barriers to employment that have been faced by many people who have the skills to work and who also have a disability. A new "diversity" group is emerging as more people with disabilities enter the workforce and employers are learning how to manage their particular needs.

What can HR do to help better integrate people with disabilities into the workforce? Diversity programs should encourage people to examine their attitudes and face any stereotypes they may have about persons with disabilities. It should increase awareness about the disability community. Once learned, these new attitudes and skills need to become part of the corporate culture. They should be implemented and practiced on a day-to-day basis and should be used to formulate organizational policies.

WHAT you need to know

Acceptance and courteous treatment of people with disabilities begins with the use of proper language. To change the way workers think about people with disabilities, it is necessary to change how they talk about them. For example, the term "handicapped" should never be used—it has negative connotations and is rejected by the disability community. Any other term that is limiting or indicates helplessness or hopelessness is also unacceptable. The accepted terminology is "a person with a disability"—it puts the emphasis on the person and not their limitations.

Diversity training

Many HR practitioners can attest that attempts to diversify the workforce may meet with resistance from the current workforce. Unfortunately, some employees view diversity as a system of preferences or quotas; it is often not perceived favorably by those who do not belong to a protected group.

Whether HR chooses to encourage cultural diversity for affirmative action reasons, business reasons or simply because it is the right thing to do, many employees might feel threatened by a diversified workforce. Therefore, organizations attempting to harness the potential of a diversified workforce may want to engage in some training and education programs to help employees understand the value in and need for diversity.

DON'T miss this

A majority of respondents to the 2001 SHRM/FORTUNE magazine survey reported that they provide diversity training for permanent employees. Forty percent reported that they had increased diversity training over the previous three years.

What type of training to offer?

The type of diversity training and education that an organization chooses to offer will necessarily depend in part on the make-up of its workforce.

Example 1: *Suppose an employer's workforce has a large segment of Hispanic or Asian workers who speak different languages and dialects. If such is the case, the organization many want to offer English as a Second Language (ESL) classes to the employees. In addition, the organization may want to sponsor supervisors and managers who volunteer to take language classes at local colleges or universities.*

Example 2: *In an organization whose workforce has a large number of older workers or newly graduated employees, HR may choose to institute mentoring programs or other kinds of programs that bring together older and younger workers and allow workers to gain from each other's experiences and knowledge.*

Group discussions and role-play. In addition to tailoring training to the workforce, there are some general training and education methods that can be employed. Many organizations show training videos to all managers and employees and have group discussions afterward. The participants are encouraged to discuss their attitudes about other groups and to examine the reasons for those attitudes and how they affect decision making and other behaviors.

In many cases, the discussion groups engage in role-playing exercises that put them in the place of members of other ethnic, racial or cultural groups. By doing this, employees can better understand the problems that another employee might have. The empathy that inevitably develops is key to successful workplace diversity.

Who's being trained? *According to a 2000 survey by William M. Mercer, 50 percent of respondents said they have mandatory diversity training for all employees, while 19 percent said training was mandatory only for managers and supervisors.*

DON'T
miss
this

Designing the program

No training program can solve workplace problems without being a part of a comprehensive effort—including policy statements, management follow-through, audits and programs to enhance employee commitment. Therefore, diversity training must be a part of a total management effort, or the training wastes resources and may be counter-productive.

Here are some recommendations to keep in mind when designing and implementing diversity training programs:

◆ **Be realistic.** It is reasonable to expect that, as a result of diversity training, there will be less resistance and backlash among the workforce and an increased commitment to the organization's goals. Do not expect diversity training to change the policies and practices of the organization. Training alone will not change the overall culture.

◆ **Get management support.** Diversity training must be championed by management at every level. There must be a genuine commitment that diversity makes good bottom-line sense. Do not start diversity training at the entry-level of the organization.

◆ **Make it part of a bigger plan.** Diversity training should be one of several initiatives to underscore corporate values and ethics, including mission and vision. Diversity should not be combined with traditional EEO/Affirmative Action training or awareness programs.

◆ **Mandate it.** Require that employees have diversity training. Do not make diversity, ethics, safety, quality or sales/product training voluntary.

◆ **Be comprehensive.** Diversity training should include the highly visible categories (gender, race and national origin) as well as the less obvious distinctions (culture, disability and education) that may operate within the organization to unfairly stigmatize individuals.

◆ **Hold people accountable.** Include a discussion of accountability in diversity training. Make clear that every employee is held responsible for his or her actions. Underscore that decisions in the workplace must be based on sound business reasons.

◆ **Evaluate and follow up.** Make sure that each session is evaluated and that there is followup after each session. Provide a way for employees to respond to training issues and discussions.

Maximizing the values of diversity

Plan ahead

Like many other HR programs, cultural diversity programs take years to effect change on a fundamental level. Many organizations may be tempted to dive in and attempt to change the way people act and believe; they think that, by doing so, they have solved the problem. This approach is a mistake that will lead to a big start for the program and a perilous end.

To really affect the culture of the organization in an attempt to accommodate ethnic sensitivity and diversity, HR must first determine why people act the way they do. Once that has been identified, the organization can take steps to modify that behavior.

Best Practices

EEOC recommends the "SPLENDID" approach

An EEOC task force published a study of best EEO practices. The task force concluded that leading companies have adopted a "SPLENDID" approach, with the "SPLENDID" acronym representing the following actions employers can take:

Study: Know the law.

Plan: Know the problems, propose solutions and develop strategies for achieving them.

Lead: Champion the cause of diversity.

Encourage: Managers and employees should encourage diversity; business practices and reward systems should reinforce that objective.

Notice: Take notice, through self-analysis, of current practices and assess progress to ensure that strategies do not cause harm or unfairness.

Discuss: Communicate and reinforce the message that diversity is a business asset and a key element to success.

Inclusion: Bring everyone into the process in the analysis, planning and implementation stages.

Dedication: Although long-term gains may cost in the short-term, invest the capital and human resources, and stay persistent.

Research

To change the corporate culture, HR must first know what it is. This may require some in-depth research in the form of a questionnaire or other surveying device. In the survey, HR will want to inquire about the employees' perceptions of how they are treated at the organization and their perceptions of how minorities as a whole are treated, among other things. Once that data has been analyzed, HR can make some determinations about how it wants to proceed.

✓ Checklist

Benchmarking against other organizations

The Department of Labor and the Office of Federal Contract Compliance Programs (OFCCP) present awards to companies that have made exemplary steps toward diversifying their workplaces and steps toward promoting equal opportunity. Here is a sampling of the kinds of activities that winners of the Opportunity 2000 and Exemplary Voluntary Effort (EVE) Awards have engaged in during past years:

- ☐ Development programs for minorities and women to propel them into management and executive positions.
- ☐ Assistance programs for disadvantaged students through minority work study programs and Adopt-A-School programs.
- ☐ Volunteer engineering program initiatives to assist individuals with disabilities by inventing devices to help them.
- ☐ Programs in collaboration with community colleges and community organizations to employ and train inner-city minorities and women for construction jobs.
- ☐ Strong internship programs that are sometimes sponsored through predominantly Hispanic or historically Black colleges.
- ☐ Urban renewal projects involving low and middle income housing and a bilingual school, in which employees are encouraged to get involved.
- ☐ Sustaining a workforce in the poorest areas of large cities.

The Quiz

1. An organization that has in place an   ❏ True   ❏ False
   anti-harassment program is successfully
   managing diversity.

2. Managing diversity does *not* include which of the following:
   a. Unifying the diverse workforce.
   b. Recognizing the differences of each employee.
   c. Disciplining employees who violate work rules.
   d. Valuing the different ideas that employees
      can bring to the organization.

3. Programs prohibiting harassment as a general   ❏ True   ❏ False
   rule focus on things to do, whereas diversity
   programs provide suggestions about things not to do.

4. According to survey data, most organizations include which of the
   following in their diversity initiatives?
   a. Race.
   b. Gender.
   c. Socioeconomic status.
   d. Both choices a and b.

5. It can take cultural diversity programs years   ❏ True   ❏ False
   to effect change on a fundamental level.

Answer key: 1.F, 2.c, 3.F, 4.d, 5.T

Index

Abuse ... *31*
Age ... *23, 178*
AIDS ... *24*
Alter-ego harassment ... *67*
Americans with Disabilities Act
    Training accommodations ... *100-101*
Audit
    best practices ... *2*

Best practices
    Audit of anti-harassment efforts ... *2*
    Communication of
        anti-harassment policy ... *95*
    Corrective action ... *158*
    Diversity ... *170-173, 176, 183*
    Equal employment
        opportunity policy ... *91-93*
    Hotline ... *85*
    Investigation ... *155*
    Knowledge by employer ... *72*
    Muslim employees ... *19*
    Office romances ... *56*
    On-line harassment ... *35*
    Supervisor harassment ... *117*
    Training ... *99-100, 105, 107*
Bias-free workplace ... *3*

Checklists
    Anti-discrimination ... *76-77*
    Complaint procedure ... *88*
    Corrective action ... *157*
    Diversity ... *174, 183*
    Examples of harassment ... *105-106*
    Gender harassment ... *20*
    Investigation of harassment
        complaint ... *90, 148, 149*
    Retaliation ... *162*
    Supervisors ... *125*
Communication of policy ... *93-95, 102*

Complaint procedure ... *83-89*
    Computer use ... *33-35*
    Corrective action ... *157*
Costs of harassment
    Hidden ... *4*
    Litigation ... *5-8*
    Settlements ... *5*
Co-worker harassment ... *73-75*

Dating in the workplace ... *52-57*
Disability ... *21*
Discrimination ... *28, 76-77*
Diversity
    Age ... *178*
    Best practices ... *172-173, 183*
    Business case ... *175*
    Checklist ... *174, 183*
    Disability ... *179-180*
    EEOC guidance ... *170-171, 183*
    Gender ... *177*
    Generally ... *168*
    Harassment prevention ... *171-172*
    Prevalence ... *173*
    Racial ... *176*
    Religion ... *178-179*
    Training ... *180-182*
    Types of programs ... *175-180*
Documentation ... *163-164*

E-mail ... *34-34*
English-only rules ... *17-18*
Equal Employment Opportunity Commission
    Investigation by ... *157*
Equal employment
    opportunity policy ... *91-93*

Failure to report harassment ... *118*
Fair Credit Reporting Act ... *137*

Gender ... *20, 177*
Glass ceiling ... *177*
Good-faith efforts ... *76*

Harassment
  Defined ... *28*
  Determining ... *29*
  Isolated instances ... *31*
Hispanics ... *15*
Hostile environment ... *28, 45*
Hotlines ... *85*

Internet ... *33*
Intimidation ... *32*
Investigation of harassment complaint
  Confidentiality ... *146-147*
  Corrective action ... *157*
  Counseling ... *153*
  Defamation ... *147-148*
  Determination ... *152-153*
  Discipline ... *160-161*
  Documentation ... *146, 163-164*
  Generally ... *89-90*
  Guidelines ... *129-138*
  Hard-to-resolve claim ... *154-155*
  Interviews ... *138-145*
  Reassignments ... *159*
  Retaliation ... *162-163*
  Transfers ... *159*

Knowledge of harassment ... *128*

Liability
  Generally ... *66*
  Managers ... *67-73*
  Supervisors ... *67-73*

Managers
  Failure to report harassment ... *118*
  Harassment by ... *116-117*
  Liability for harassment ... *67-73*
  Responsibilities of ... *118-125*

Tolerance of harassment ... *49*
Training ... *102, 108-110*
Marital status ... *24*
Muslim employees ... *19*

National origin ... *15*
Non-employee harassment ... *37-38, 75*
Non-minorities ... *19*

Office romances ... *52-57*

Parenthood ... *24*
Physical threats ... *32*
Policy against harassment
  Advantages ... *80*
  Communication ... *93-95*
  Complaint procedures ... *83-86*
  Examples of prohibited conduct ... *82*
  Key provisions ... *80-81*
  Worst case scenario ... *87*
Pregnancy ... *24*
Protected traits
  Federal law ... *14*
Punitive damages ... *76*

Race ... *15-16*
Reassignments ... *159*
Religion ... *21, 178-179*
Retaliation ... *71, 88-89, 162-163*

Sexual harassment
  Compliments ... *47*
  Examples ... *47, 106*
  Generally ... *42*
  Hostile environment ... *45*
  Isolated instances ... *48*
  Quid pro quo ... *50*
  Same-sex harassment ... *51*
  Sexual orientation harassment ... *51-52*
  State law ... *57-62*
  Tangible job actions ... *50, 69*
  Tolerated behavior ... *44*

Unwelcome sexual conduct ... *43*
  Worst case scenario ... *49*
Sexual preference ... *24*
State laws
  Sexual harassment ... *57-62*
Supervisors
  Failure to report harassment ... *118*
  Harassment by ... *116-117*
  Liability for harassment ... *67-73*
  Responsibilities of ... *118-125*
  Tolerance of harassment ... *49*
  Training ... *102, 108-110*
  Worst case scenario ... *119-120*

Tangible job action ... *69*
Third-party harassment ... *37-38, 75*
Threats ... *32*
Training
  Americans with Disabilities Act ... *100-101*
  Benefits of ... *98*
  Best practices ... *99-100. 105, 107*
  Communication ... *102*
  Components ... *101-108*

Diversity ... *180-182*
Documentation ... *110-111*
Evaluation ... *111-112*
General ... *102*
Legal reasons ... *99*
Regular training ... *101*
Supervisors ... *102*
Transfers ... *159*

Verbal threats ... *32*
Veteran status ... *23*
Vicarious liability ... *68*

Worst case scenario
  Customer harassment ... *38*
  Investigation ... *165*
  Manager's harassment ... *69, 119-120*
  Mental disability ... *22*
  Policy against harassment ... *87*
  Racial complaints ... *16*
  Religion complaints ... *21*
  Sexual harassment ... *49*